What People are Saying About *¡Visión!*

One of the least well known engines of our recent record economic prosperity is the Hispanic entrepreneur. Hispanic-owned businesses are among the fastest growing type of small business in the United States and not only are they creating wealth, they are revitalizing neighborhoods and building communities. ¡Visión! could not be timelier in reporting on, and analyzing the impact of, one of the most phenomenal trends in the Latino community of the last decade.

Raúl Yzaguirre, President and CEO
National Council of la RAZA

Every reader's personal vision will be inspired and guided by the stories of how others turned their aspirations into reality.

Sandra Hernandez Adams, President-Elect
National Association of Women Business Owners

This book pulls together a wealth of information about a growing segment of the economy – Hispanic entrepreneurs – and then brings the statistics to life with compelling personal stories of struggle and success. A unique addition to entrepreneurship literature.

Kurt Mueller, President,
Kauffman Center for Entrepreneurial Leadership
The Ewing Marion Kauffman Foundation

An interesting compendium of entrepreneurs who played key roles in the development of Hispanic enterprise economy during the last 25 years of the 20th century. The biographical data are particularly arresting ...

Dr. Jesús Chavarría, CEO
Hispanic Business

The next great American business success story will be a woman ... and she undoubtedly will be Hispanic.

Amy J. Millman, Executive Director
National Women's Business Council

Mabel Tinjacá has done an absolutely wonderful job on this topic, Hispanic entrepreneurship in America. Entrepreneurs come in all genders and ethnicities. The people mentioned by Mabel are not only role models for the Hispanic community but for all American citizens. I sincerely applaud her outstanding work!

Steven Rogers, Professor
Kellogg School of Business

From Dr. Mabel Tinjacá's studies of the processes of entrepreneurship and the development of robust communities has emerged a groundbreaking publication that frames the best practices of truly successful Hispanic entrepreneurs. The individuals depicted are the leaders of today and tomorrow, whose concerns drive the future of the nation's economy. These leaders may represent a minority of the U.S. population, but they demonstrate the power of numbers and represent the vigor and enterprise that distinguishes the American character.

George Herrera, President and CEO
U.S. Hispanic Chamber of Commerce

We all know the premium a college education places on family income and on a better life for our children. These stories will help our children see what is possible when they persist.

Sara Martinez Tucker, President and CEO
Hispanic Scholarship Fund

Mabel Tinjacá shows, through stories of successful Hispanic entrepreneurs, that gender, family and community issues play an important role in the success of new ventures. This book is a must for those contemplating a business venture and is critical for those questioning their own ability to create and grow a successful business.

Dr. Donald L. Sexton, Professor Emeritus
Ohio State University

Mike & Karen

My best wishes

to you. Thank you

Mabel

January 23, 2001

¡Visión!

Hispanic Entrepreneurs
in the United States

Compliments of

KAUFFMAN CENTER
FOR ENTREPRENEURIAL LEADERSHIP
AT THE EWING MARION KAUFFMAN FOUNDATION

Mabel
1-23-01

Mabel Tinjacá, Ph.D.

¡Visión!

Hispanic Entrepreneurs in the United States

MABEL TINJACÁ, PH.D.

¡Querer es Poder!
Where there is a will there is a way!

Preface by
Solomon D. Trujillo, Former CEO
U.S. WEST

Heritage Publishing Company
Pleasant Hill, Missouri

Publisher's Cataloging-in-Publication

Tinjacá, Mabel
    ¡Visión! Hispanic Entrepreneurs in the United States /
    Mabel Tinjacá. – 1st ed.
    Includes bibliographical references and index.
    LCCN: 00134220
    ISBN: 0-9672363-1-2

    1. Hispanic American businesspeople. 2. Hispanic
American business enterprises. 3. Entrepreneurship –
United States. I. Title. II. Title: Hispanic entrepreneurs
in the United States

    HD2346.U5T56 2000   658.02′2′08968
                                        QBI00-841

Reach for the Stars
©2001 by Gabriel Nieto

Cover and Interior Design by Tappan Design

    This publication was funded by the Kauffman Center for Entrepreneurial Leadership at the Ewing Marion Kauffman Foundation, Kansas City, Missouri. The contents and views expressed herein are solely those of the author.

To Clara Inéz Vargas

Acknowledgments

Writing a book is a team effort. It certainly was the case for *¡Visión!* Many busy and very generous people contributed a significant amount of their time and effort to this project. Many more gave referrals, offered names and made personal contacts to secure interviews with some of the most influential and successful Hispanic CEOs in the United States. These entrepreneurs offered their life stories hoping that others could benefit from their experiences.

The entrepreneurs highlighted in *¡Visión!* reviewed drafts and sustained the lengthy process of writing and rewriting the manuscript. I would like to thank all of them for their tremendous contribution and hope that their gift will have the intended effect of encouraging others to engage their talents in the entrepreneurial process, in community development and in philanthropy.

I would like to add a special note of appreciation to the Ewing Marion Kauffman Foundation in Kansas City, Missouri. Its founder, Mr. K., strongly believed that community development happens best when the social and economic pieces work together. The foundation's vision statement "to develop self-sufficient people in healthy communities" reflects his personal vision for emerging communities. I had many "Mr. K. moments" while researching and writing this manuscript.

I had the support of a tremendous advisory board – Rhonda Holman, Siobon Nicholau, Steven Rogers, Steve Roling, Donald Sexton, Ray Smilor and Gene Wilson – whose suggestions improved the manuscript tremendously. I felt continually blessed to have an editor, Susan Herold, who edits in both English and Spanish. My production editors, Roseanne Wickman, and Kirsten McBride were also wonderful. Pola Firestone, my publicist, helped tremendously to make sure this manuscript was both credible and viable.

My husband, Will O. Tucker, and my son, Christopher, who are such important parts of my life, kept me grounded and inspired throughout this lengthy process. The support of my family and friends meant so much to me, especially when writing late at night, fretting over the same paragraph for the ninteenth time and then wondering – Is this any good?

Family and friends … could anyone ask for more? There are many others, too numerous to mention, who are encouraging self-sufficiency for healthy communities and who also took time for this project. Thank you all.

Finally, I know I had help from the Grand Master Planner because of how blessed this project has been. Truly, all things happen for a reason. I have heard over and over that the sharing, the camaraderie and the learning made this a unique experience for many people who involved themselves in the project. That was certainly the case for me. Last, thank you, the reader. I hope you find reading this book as rewarding as it was to write it.

Table of Contents

¡Visión!
Hispanic Entrepreneurs
in the United States

Preface by Solomon D. Trujillo

When you work in the world of technology as I do, you live and breathe predictions. In that kind of atmosphere, you learn very quickly to sort the realistic from the fantastical, to weigh and balance the possible against the probable. But as Mabel Tinjacá so skillfully explores in ¡Vision! Hispanic Entrepreneurs in the United States, it doesn't take a whole lot of imagination or careful analysis to conclude that for America, the 21st century will be a time of profoundly expanding Hispanic influence – in our social structures, in the political arena and, maybe most important, in business.

Hispanics are a large and growing part of the American dream. That's important, because numbers count in a democracy because people vote. And numbers count in business because people buy things. The combination of growing political power and growing economic power translates into growing influence that will some day be equal to the sheer number of Hispanics themselves.

By 2010, experts predict that Hispanics will be the largest minority group in the United States with more than 20 percent of the nation's population. Our Hispanic population by itself will be larger than that of most of America's trading partners. In a nation governed by the principles of democratic capitalism, those numbers represent a tremendous opportunity – an opportunity not just for Hispanics but for all Americans.

It is an opportunity Hispanics are poised to take, because their success in the world of business is well established. I'm not talking only about those Hispanic leaders who have made it to the boardroom or the executive suite of large, multinational corporations, but rather about the explosion of Hispanic-owned, Hispanic-*started* businesses. These are the true growth engines of our economy. From fewer than a half million Hispanic-owned businesses just five years ago, we have grown to the point where there are now 2 million. By any standard, that rate of growth is phenomenal.

In Los Angeles county alone, Latino-owned firms increased by 700 percent over the last two decades – three times the over-all Latino population growth! Hispanics are creating businesses at *three times* the rate of the rest of the population. Latinas are starting new businesses at *four times* that rate. No other group even comes close.

These numbers don't surprise me in the least because of my personal experience. A number of years ago, I was the founding president of a group called the U S WEST Small Business Group. It was easy even then to predict the spectacular rise of Hispanic businesses, because every time I went out to meet customers, I found hard-working Hispanic entrepreneurs who were imbued with the desire to create wealth in a free-enterprise system that rewarded effort and initiative.

Some of these businesspersons were what I call "Pilgrims" – people just looking for a new way of life. They weren't trying to start the next Wal-Mart or Microsoft or Exxon. They were just try-ing to make a better living for themselves and their families ... to buy a home, to send their kids to a community college or the state university, to take care of their parents ... because those aspira-tions are important to our community.

I also encountered a few hard chargers. These I called "Swashbucklers." They were going to change the world, create new markets and get rich.

Whether the people I met were Pilgrims or Swashbucklers, they had in common a strong work ethic and shared a culture that values learning, loyalty, performance and personal respon-sibility. Guess what? These are precisely the qualities that are required to win in the New Economy. I believe this is why our community is doing so well by any standard.

It's easy when you read the business pages of the daily newspaper to equate business with *big* business. Microsoft will always make more headlines than the accountants in the office next door or the car dealer down the street. But this kind of attention masks the fact that of the 22 million business enterprises in the United States, only 14,000 have more than 500 employees. The other 21 million plus are sole proprietorships, partnerships and small and mid-sized businesses. These are the businesses that sponsor the soccer teams and underwrite the Fourth of July parade and hire our children for summer jobs.

And this is a world where Hispanics have already succeeded. I, for one, am optimistic that the success we've enjoyed is merely prelude to the greater success that is in store for Hispanic business.

Why? The Department of Commerce reports that half of U.S. exports measured by *dollar value* are now achieved by companies with fewer than 500 employees. If you measure exports by the size of the company doing the exporting, you'll see that 50 percent of our exports are by companies with fewer than 100 employees. In some Western states, it's higher than 80 percent.

Hispanic businesses have a new and powerful tool in the Internet. The Internet has the unique ability to make a small business look large – to level a playing field that has been too often tilted. Are Hispanics taking advantage of this promise? The answer is "yes" and "no."

Compared with the rest of the population, Hispanics are more likely to use the Internet for travel ... e-mail ... online shopping ... chat rooms ... more likely to use it for news ... entertainment ... education ... business and finance ... more likely to use the Internet for all those things than the rest of the population. In fact, the only area where Hispanics use the Internet less than the rest of the population is for information about sports.

From 1984 to 1994, the Hispanic adult population in the United States gained access to computers at a rate twice as fast as the rest of the population.

Over that same period of time, their Internet usage increased by 650 percent. Yahoo! launched a Spanish-language Web service in 1999 that began with about 5,000 Spanish-language Web sites. At last count, it had more than 27,000 sites.

And 30 percent of Hispanic households now own computers – two and a half times more than owned computers just five years ago. When asked if they agree with the statement, "I go out of my way to learn about and make use of devices, methods and products that represent advanced technologies," Hispanics agreed by a factor of two to one.

Hispanics who have embraced the Information Age have done so with unmatched enthusiasm.

These facts take on added importance when you consider that in just seven years, the University of Texas predicts that fully half of the workers in America will be employed in the information technology industry. A June 2000 study showed that the number of people employed in Internet-related jobs doubled in the last year alone.

For Hispanics to create more success stories such as the ones Dr. Mabel Tinjacá presents in these pages, we should ask ourselves, Will we and our children be prepared? Will we have the skills to compete for high-technology jobs? And will we have the kind of high-speed access to the Internet that is a prerequisite to enable e-business, e-commerce, distance learning and all the other applications embedded in the 'net?

In short, will we live in the world of *possibility*, or will we live in the world of *probability*?

No one can answer that authoritatively, because the Information Age has once again taught us the bitter lesson that *una cosa es prometer, otra es cumplir* (It is one thing to promise and another to fulfill).

Today, in the midst of the Information Age, whites are three times more likely to have access to the Internet than African-Americans or Hispanics. A white, two-parent household earning less than $35,000 a year is nearly *four times* more likely to have Internet access than a Hispanic household making the same amount of money.

So we have challenges, yes. But we have always had challenges. The pages that follow show real examples, real people, real progress.

Dr. Tinjacá begins with an overview of the state of Hispanics in America that will provide new and eye-opening information for even the most informed among us. Once she's provided that global view, she takes us into the lives of six Hispanics who have made their dreams come true.

At the beginning of the last century, Americans were fascinated with the fictional Horatio Alger success stories. At the beginning of this century, the stories Dr. Tinjacá presents would stretch the abilities of even the most imaginative novelist. These are stories of challenges met and challenges overcome. The people you will meet here have lives that are inspirational, emotional, and have remarkably similar patterns, which Dr. Tinjacá identifies in "Leadership Lessons and Best Practices."

Dr. Tinjacá has given us a work of far-reaching importance. It is full of valuable information that corporations, Hispanic entrepreneurs, academics and government and community leaders can only ignore at their own risk, because in telling the stories of others, she has given us a script for ourselves.

Her important work deserves our attention.

Solomon D. Trujillo
Former CEO, U.S. WEST
Denver, Colorado

PART I

THE
EMERGENCE
OF HISPANIC
ENTREPRENEURS

CHAPTER ONE

¡VISIÓN!
INTRODUCTION

B etween 1955 and 1965, six young Hispanics were preparing for their entrepreneurial journeys. Tom Vélez was taking violin lessons under the watchful eye of his father in the South Bronx. Nancy Archuleta, perched in the branches of her backyard willow tree, was contemplating a future among the stars as an astronomer. Danny Villanueva was making his move from professional football to Spanish language television in southern California. Teresa McBride was preparing mistletoe bunches for sale in Grants, New Mexico. Carlos Saladrigas was selling shoes and purses from the handlebars of his moped in Miami so he could save enough money to help his parents get a new start when they left Cuba. And Anna Cablik was crossing swollen rivers on horseback in Panama on her way home from school.

In the years that followed, they all went to school or to work, met difficult challenges and acquired experiences that helped them start and lead some of the most innovative and successful companies in the United States. Some of them not only started businesses but helped start new industries. They represent the hundreds of thousands of Hispanic entrepreneurs who quietly, persistently and successfully worked hard for many years to realize their vision for a better future.

It was during the decade between 1955 and 1965 that analysts with the U.S. Census Bureau began noticing upward trends in most of their demographic studies. The growth trends were strong and undeniable. The 1980 Census report discussing these trends became the source of many articles, appearing mostly in Hispanic magazines.

In the late 1980s, articles about this emerging market began appearing in magazines like *American Demographics* that are popular among marketing professionals. More recently, academic journals in sociology and social public policy have begun publishing articles about ethnic and immigrant entrepreneurship that describe the effects of these demographic trends on the world of business and on community development.

In 1984, Richard G. Arellano, with the help of a task force of prominent business leaders, researched and wrote *Strategies for Hispanic Business Development*, published by the National Chamber Foundation (NCF) of the United States Chamber of Commerce (USCC).[1]

Several years earlier, William Verity, then CEO of Armco and chairman of the USCC, had met Hector Barreto, Sr. president of the new U.S. Hispanic Chamber of Commerce (USHCC). During their many conversations about the Hispanic business community, Mr. Verity decided to commission research about Hispanic entrepreneurs. As Mr. Barreto comments, Mr. Verity thought "it was high time that the rest of the American business community recognized the skill and importance of its Hispanic colleagues and began cooperative efforts aimed at helping Hispanic business reach its destiny as a major force in the U.S. economy."[2]

Arellano's comprehensive and well-researched volume remains a well-known secret – somewhat known within the Hispanic business community and a secret to the rest of the business community. The foreword, written by Walter G. Smith, who was executive director of the Armco Foundation at the time, exhorted the American business community, the Hispanic business community and the various levels of government to "not let the promise of this report go unfulfilled."

But the idea that a small minority – Spanish-speaking, portrayed as lazy or as gangsters or as merely Latin lovers by the media – would soon change the cultural milieu of the United States, or that salsa would outsell ketchup, or that Hispanics would contribute to the financial standing of the largest economic power in the world, may have seemed far-fetched in 1984.

The promise of the Hispanic business community was inevitable and is becoming a reality today. Hispanics – too many to be ignored – began their businesses as a way of supporting their loved ones and then grew them to fulfill their personal visions. Often this was the only choice they had, because they were denied jobs in corporations and government or because business ownership was a natural choice for them. In other cases, the inevitability sprang from successful businesses that were a source of family pride and were passed on to following generations. The reasons varied but the outcome was a significant demographic trend toward increased prosperity for a growing minority.

With the growth of Hispanic businesses came the growth of communities and the development of increasing numbers of young leaders. They were getting educations and gradually assuming leading roles in corporations, governments and nonprofit organizations. The media began to take notice of a growing list of Hispanic firsts, adding to a lengthy list dating back to the 1500s, according to Nicolás Kanellos.[3]

In 1959, Severo Ochoa became the first U.S. Hispanic winner of the Nobel Prize in medicine for his synthesis of RNA. Luis Walter Alvarez was the first U.S.-born Hispanic to win the Nobel Prize in physics in 1968. Ramona Acosta Bañuelos was the first Hispanic U.S. Treasurer, appointed in 1972, and Edward Hidalgo was appointed the first Hispanic U.S. Secretary of the Navy in 1979.

The 1980s produced additional firsts: Franklin Chang-Diaz was the first Hispanic in space; Lauro F. Cavazos was the first Hispanic appointed U.S. Secretary of Education; Antonia Coello Novello of Puerto Rico was the first woman and Hispanic U.S. Surgeon General. Modesto (Mitch) Maidique became the first Cuban-American president of a major university when he took over Florida International University in 1986.

The list of firsts became even longer in the 1990s. Henry G. Cisneros was the first Hispanic U.S. Secretary of Housing and Urban Development. Federico F. Peña was the first Hispanic Secretary of Transportation and later the first Secretary of Energy. Oscar Hijuelos was the first Hispanic American novelist to win the Pulitzer Prize for fiction in 1991, for *The Mambo Kings Play Songs of Love*. Mario J. Molina, a Hispanic, shared the Nobel Prize in chemistry for work that influenced an international ban on chemicals believed to deplete the ozone layer.

Corporate CEO and presidential firsts also made the news. Roberto C. Goizueta at Coca-Cola, Carlos Jose Arboleya at Barnett Banks of Miami, Katherine D. Ortega at Santa Ana State Bank, Frank Alonzo at Continental Airlines, and Carlos M.Gutierrez at Kellogg Co. were among the first Hispanics to occupy lofty corporate slots.

Despite this growing list of firsts, Hispanic communities with limited access to resources continue to struggle, especially in the areas of education and health services. But the hard work of civil rights, education, government and business leaders who preceded the current generation of Hispanics and other minorities is paying off. A strong economy has also contributed to business and community development. This window of opportunity stands a good chance of benefiting all and demonstrates the importance of capitalizing on strengths while addressing limitations.

This book hopes to take the promise discussed in Arellano's *Strategies for Hispanic Business Development* and present it again to the American business community, this time as a business opportunity. It sets out to offer this opportunity to the Hispanic community as an acknowledgment of the courage, strength of character and business savvy of entrepreneurs who have not had time or who were too modest to bring attention to themselves in this way. This book presents their persistent vision of a better future for Hispanic communities.

Now is a different time. The millennium as a worldwide milestone encourages reflection, reevaluation and the formation of a new vision. The tables and projections in the U.S. Census statistical reports, the Economic Census Reports, marketing and sociology research and business articles reflect important national trends – from music to food, from the amazing proliferation of Hispanic firms to partnerships between major U.S. Fortune 500 companies and international Hispanic-owned companies. Perhaps now is simply a better time to make known their vision.

The word *visión* carries the force of conviction and the power of ambition. Its English connotation is inspirational. In Spanish, pronounced "vee zion," it is almost electric, perhaps because its accent creates emphasis at the end of the word, giving it a spark of determination. With exclamation points added, this word captures the entrepreneurial energy that characterizes the current proliferation of Hispanic businesses in the United States – ¡Visión!

This phenomenon is framed by the rise of Hispanics as a social, economic and political force in the United States. The increasing prosperity of this community is reflected in its purchasing power, its wealth creation and its political empowerment. The 35 million Hispanics who reside in the United States and Puerto Rico have a purchasing power of $360 billion. As consumers, they stand among the nation's largest trading partners, exceeding Canada, Japan and Mexico.

The challenges to the continued growth and success of this community may seem daunting but the future looks promising. The number of Hispanics graduating from college continues to increase while the high school dropout rate – currently much too high – continues to decline. And as the Hispanic middle class continues to grow, Hispanics steadily increase their leadership presence in corporate, government and nonprofit organizations.

Now the fastest growing labor market in the United States, well-prepared Hispanic high school and college graduates are a future asset for mainstream businesses and an essential component of Hispanic businesses. This is especially true for firms facing increasing demands for fully bilingual employees.

Now it is also the fastest growing business community – no other area of economic life in the United States compares to the 305 percent growth in Hispanic businesses. All other businesses have experienced only 26 percent growth. The most conservative estimate of annual receipts for the 1.5 million Hispanic-owned businesses is $184 billion. This represents a 400 percent increase in revenues since 1987.

The most obvious Hispanic influence is on American popular culture. Latino music, food and styles are capturing the heart of the mainstream consumer. The new millennium unfolds with a Hispanic flair as the influence of this group on both America's economy and its social fabric widens, merges with other influences and redefines American culture.

One of the strengths of the Hispanic community is its heterogeneity – it is many communities with distinct histories and cultures. Language, ethnic pride and shared values have created emotional links that have strengthened the bonds of a homeland within the United States. And this is the defining common denominator for Hispanics. Diversity and national pride remain but the U.S. connection is fundamental.

Rich Past

From the beginning, Hispanic entrepreneurs have helped shape the economic, cultural and social milieu of the United

States. Theirs has been a colorful, highly textured and unique contribution to American society. This comes from a diversity that has defined how Hispanics approach family, business and community, the way they distribute wealth and how they relate to government.

From the early days of the United States, Spanish influence has colored the contributions of explorers, pioneers and merchants throughout a vast portion of this land. Like other European explorers, the Spanish abrogated the rights of native peoples in establishing their own settlements. They converted the land to vast cattle ranches and, in so doing, left a wide mark from California to the Southwest, Texas and Florida. The communities that grew up in these areas remain strong today. International trade with the original 13 colonies, with Caribbean islands and with Spain, the mother country, had its start with the cattle industry.

The history following the initial exploration and expansion by Europeans in the New World is marked by wars – wars waged against the Native Americans, wars with rival European powers, and wars of independence. As Spain lost its New World lands to other European powers and then to the United States, the latter gained an immeasurable benefit. Large numbers of Hispanics became U.S. citizens.

The new citizens, brought into the Union through the Treaty of Hidalgo, arrived in the growing republic with already established entrepreneurial communities based on ranching. While many Hispanics lost their land, those who managed to retain it continued the ranching tradition. In the ensuing decades, wars for independence in the Caribbean and Central and South America brought more Hispanic immigrants to the United States in search of greater opportunity.

The U.S. civil rights movement and the country's war in Southeast Asia were times of profound change for all Americans. Hispanic Americans, in particular, saw a demand for equal educational opportunities as well as equal rights. As the community worked to resolve these issues, the stage was set for better education and opportunities for succeeding generations of Hispanic citizens. Progress may have seemed slow, but it was steady, and from these efforts emerged a group of entrepreneurs that complemented the growing community of Hispanics throughout the United States.

The statistics reflected the reality of this growth, but the increasing purchasing power of the community and the tremendous growth of its businesses caught the attention of demographers and sociologists. Soon corporations saw Hispanics as new markets, business partners and employees.

Rich Present

Today the picture is that of an economic renaissance, with Hispanic businesses growing in numbers, complexity and scope. Leading this surge are the Latinas – Hispanic women who, like their enterprising ancestors, have elected self-determination over waiting for business and society to acknowledge their worth.

The renaissance is apparent in community growth and the prosperity fueled by the zeal for betterment that is part of the immigrant culture. This zeal manifests itself in an ever-present acknowledgment of the possible and a faith in the potential of the individual to make a difference. The renaissance has made itself known through hard work and the resulting contributions to a very robust U.S. economy. The interplay between business success and community growth is an essential activity that Hispanic entrepreneurs have fostered. Their contribution in this arena has been quiet and steady and is the reason why Aida Alvarez, head of the Small Business Administration, calls them America's "unsung heroes."

These heroes started out with a ¡visión! for family security, which grew into something bigger than just successful businesses. Their vision will leave an ultimate legacy, a representation of themselves in a way that brings wealth and health to families, communities, industry, the nation and the world. The six entrepreneurs featured in this book exemplify this vision, and their success accrues to everyone.

Successful Hispanic entrepreneurs are role models. They provide jobs and help families create wealth. Through their leadership in their communities, they prove the importance of education, hard work, philanthropy and community service. They help build community infrastructures and, through their involvement in the political process, they promote community power bases. Through their philanthropic emphasis on building community and leaving legacies, they provide much more than economic stability – they help build healthy communities.

Richer Future

As the present gives way to the future and the new millennium prompts introspection, Hispanic entrepreneurs increasingly set their sights on globalization. This complex and lucrative area of commerce is ready-made for businesspeople who are sensitive to and value cultural differences, are used to relationship-based business practices and understand the intricacies of international commerce. They will evaluate, minimize, plan for and address the risks because this is, after all, what entrepreneurs do well.

While significant challenges remain for Hispanics that will undoubtedly affect all Americans – minority or otherwise – this young, growing and increasingly "ready" minority continues to forge ahead. Hispanic leaders and entrepreneurs will play a significant part in developing a vision that resonates with all young people, not just young Hispanics.

Thus, the lists of "firsts" will continue to grow; the promise and the demographic projections will become a reality for Hispanic groups and for Hispanic businesses; and the legacy cycle of philanthropy and community development will continue from child to child.

"The last two decades have been a time during which Hispanics have constructed the stage on which their story will be played out in future generations," according to Bill Richardson, U.S. Secretary of Energy.[4] The opportunity and the promise are the *¡visión!* of tomorrow that has begun today.

Notes

[1]No longer in print. Richard Arellano, *Strategies for Hispanic Business Development* (Washington, DC, National Chamber Foundation (NCF) of the United States Chamber of Commerce, 1984).

[2]Richard Arellano, Strategies for Hispanic Business Development (Washington, DC, National Chamber Foundation (NCF) of the United States Chamber of Commerce, 1984).

[3]Nicolás Kanello, *Hispanic Firsts: 500 Years of Extraordinary Achievements* (Houston, Texas: Arte Público Press, 1997).

[4]*Hispanic Business*, "The Hispanic Century." *Hispanic Business*. (1999) April, 21.

CHAPTER TWO

A
POWERFUL
FORCE

Purchasing power, wealth creation and political empowerment are positioning the Hispanic community as a powerful force in the United States. The beginning of the millennium is unfolding with a Hispanic flair as their influence on the American economy and social fabric widens, merges and redefines a new American culture.

It may look like pop culture has suddenly gone Latino. Charles Gonzales, author of *Yes You Can: Every Latino's Guide to Building Family Wealth,* writes the most vivid description of how Hispanic culture is making its mark on America. "Throughout all the islands of Hispanic America, business booms and night life pulsates to Latin rhythms; Latin fashion, food and music drive a new American pop culture. Highly mobile Latino populations overflow their inner-city roots; each year, the latest Latino additions to middle-class America move to the suburbs."[1]

The Hispanics' stories are often about difficult social and political realities. Some came to the United States to provide stability for their families. Others came for asylum, and yet others were forced from their homelands. They built new lives and became part of a new country. Some Hispanics already were residents of North America and the Caribbean generations before the Mexican-American and the Spanish-American Wars changed their national governments. As a result, they have a different story to tell.

Today's demographics show both the phenomenal growth in purchasing power, wealth creation and political empowerment and the significant challenges that the Hispanic community continues to face. These strengths and challenges affect all Americans, given the political, social and economic realities of the broader U.S. demographics.

But it does not stop there. Within the context of the Americas, Hispanics continue to play an important role as contributors to international trade, as interested parties to democracy and as family members with cultural ties to one or more Latino countries. With partnerships in the Americas and economic interests in globalization, Hispanics are becoming strong players in the world market. Thus, what defines Hispanics and how they lead their day-to-day lives is of vital importance to us all.

Purchasing Power

Hispanics are the fastest-growing consumer and workforce segment in the United States. The wealth of the nation's 35 million Hispanics is growing at three times the rate of inflation.[2] According to the National Council of la RAZA, it was approximately $350 billion in 1997, which represents an increase of 66 percent since 1990.[3] The Selig Center for Economic Growth at the University of Georgia estimated Hispanic purchasing power at $383 billion in 1999.[4] This puts the U.S. Hispanic market on a par with the nation's largest trading partners, surpassing Canada, Japan and Mexico in terms of purchasing power.[5]

Between 1990 and 1999, U.S. Hispanics' purchasing power increased by 84 percent and is expected to grow to $1 trillion by 2010, according to the same University of Georgia report.

Anna Escobedo Cabral, president and CEO of the Hispanic Association on Corporate Responsibility (HACR), estimates that Hispanic buying power increases by $1 billion every three weeks and would approach $400 billion by December 1999. The Hispanic community is young, growing and upwardly mobile, and these figures only begin to describe their potential power in the marketplace.[6]

Wealth Creation and Entrepreneurship

Wealth has been created in Hispanic communities in large part through entrepreneurship and increased levels of education. The most affluent 50 to 80 families of the Hispanic population saw its wealth increase from $2.3 billion to $9.3 billion in just six years (1991-1997), as reported by *Hispanic Business* magazine.[7] More than 70 percent of the Hispanic Rich List reported by *Hispanic Business* acquired or grew their wealth through business ownership, technology services, engineering, finance, investment banking, real estate development and construction. The 25 percent considered "old money" has also involved entrepreneurship.[8]

Charles Gonzales comments:

The emergence of literally millions of affluent Latinos over the last twenty-five years is one of the great demographic events in modern America: nearly one-half of all Latinos are already middle class, and nearly one-half of those are affluent. But is has been a stealth event. While the so-called experts were wondering if Latinos would ever cease being poor, many of us quietly, and without massive government assistance, did the hard work that put us into the affluent category.[9]

A strong family culture and increasing levels of education support the trend away from poverty. A study by Gregory Rodriguez of Pepperdine University concluded that Hispanic residents of southern California are pooling resources, working their way out of poverty and steadily and solidly moving into the middle class. Rodriguez found that Hispanic families are the largest purchasers of homes.

Further, Rodriguez found that the longer Hispanic immigrants reside in the United States, the more likely they are to enter the middle class, and that U.S.-born children and grandchildren of Hispanic immigrants fare considerably better than all immigrants.[10]

According to *Hispanic Business*, 5 percent of Hispanics earned between $75,000 and $100,000 in 1997. The proportion earning $100,000 or more jumped from 2.1 percent to 4.1 percent, gaining the attention of high-end goods and services companies.[11] And the number of Hispanic households with aggregated annual incomes exceeding $75,000 had climbed to about 9.1 percent in 1997 compared with 6 percent in 1980.[12]

The highest concentration of middle-class and affluent Hispanics can be found outside regions with traditionally high Hispanic populations. Therefore the proportion of Hispanic households with income greater than $50,000 is highest in parts of northern Alaska and in rural counties throughout the eastern United States whereas wealth in California, Texas and Florida is more dispersed. Los Angeles County has an estimated 234,000 Hispanic households with annual incomes over $50,000.

By 1990 there were nearly four times as many households composed of U.S.-born Hispanics in the middle class as there were at the poverty level, and more than 58.6 percent of these middle-class households earned more than $50,000 annually.[13] The U.S. Department of Housing and Urban Development reports that home ownership among Hispanics increased from 39.4 percent to 44.7 percent between 1993 and 1998. And of the estimated 2.2 million households headed by foreign-born citizens expected to become homeowners between 1995 and 2010, 48 percent will be Hispanic, according to a Harvard University report.

Wealth creation has traditionally been viewed as a result of entrepreneurial activity. This is also true for the Hispanic community. The dramatic rise in entrepreneurial success has changed the lives and standing of many Hispanics. Further, the entrepreneurial trend appears to be strengthening as Hispanics start, grow and harvest companies at record speeds. This will be discussed further in Chapter 3.

Creating wealth within minority communities means much more than attaining affluence. Many writers about African-American entrepreneurship, such as Timothy Mason Bates and Robert Lee Wallace, have reported on economic self-sufficiency through entrepreneurship and its importance to minority communities. In essence, creating community wealth means creating and attaining a political and economic power base – it means participating fully "at the table" as a contributing member when important decisions are made that affect the community and social policy in general. This kind of political power revitalizes communities.

In particular, creating wealth through entrepreneurship means creating jobs. To a minority community, jobs represent opportunity – opportunity to access quality education, health care and housing. Thus, as social activism yielded social programs essential to the survival of minorities in need, the economic piece of the community development puzzle presents itself through entrepreneurship.

This combination of social, economic and political activity creates self-sufficiency and strength; it is, fundamentally, what makes entrepreneurs and entrepreneurship important, especially within minority communities. This makes the life stories of the successful Hispanic entrepreneurs featured in Chapters 4 through 9 compelling. They are the tip of the iceberg. More effort should be placed on highlighting entrepreneurial community leaders – especially those who advocate ethical business practices and actively participate in the betterment of the community.

Political Empowerment

Participation in the democratic process is the underlying activity that supports the ability to create wealth and increase purchasing power. Political involvement and empowerment enable Hispanics to participate fully in social policy formation. The Hispanic agenda has become a national political agenda with issues of immigration, affirmative action and education weighing heavily in voters' decisions. These are only some of the political interests of Hispanics, however. The large Hispanic entrepreneurial community places great importance on Constitutional rights, taxes, education, health care, social security, community development and international commerce.

Hispanics are becoming a stronger political force with each election, especially presidential elections. According to a Univisión Communication, Inc. report, 16 million Hispanic adults in nine states account for 83 percent of all Hispanics.[14] This concentration can have a definite effect on the outcome of elections. The four Hispanic "mega" states, California, Texas, New York and Florida, have growing populations who are choosing to vote. In California alone 1 million new Hispanic voters have registered to vote since the last presidential election.

Further, 2.2 million legal immigrants are eligible to apply for citizenship. This is important because according to the Census Bureau, naturalized Hispanic citizens are more likely to vote than native-born Hispanics. With the recent immigration policy reforms and the National Voter Registration Act (NVRA), which makes registration easier, there will likely be many new registered voters who actually vote in California.

The three other states – Texas, Florida and New York – also reflected an increase in state elections between 1992 and 1996. For example, the number of Latinos voting in Texas increased from 13.6 to 17.1 percent; in New York, from 5 to 7.5 percent; and in Florida, from 7.1 to 9.2 percent.

Juan Andrade, Jr. points out that the gains recorded between 1992 and 1996, when 1 million more – an increase of 19 percent – turned out to vote, challenge the perception of Hispanics as "the sleeping giant."[15] During the 1996 election, about 5 million of 6.6 million registered Hispanic voters cast their votes in the national elections.[16] This was a record turnout for the community and accounted for 5 percent of the total national turnout, the highest ever.

Not only are more Hispanics voting, fewer non-Hispanics are voting.[17] Nationwide, voting by non-Hispanics decreased by 8.7 percent between 1992 and 1996. That put the number of non-Hispanics casting votes in the presidential election at 95.3 percent in 1996, compared with 96.3 percent in 1992. This also adds significance to the Hispanic vote.

Yet according to the Census Bureau, Hispanic voters have held steady in the last two presidential elections, when over-all percentages are taken into account. The significance of this trend can be appreciated within the context of current demo-graphic and voting trends. First, according to the Census Bureau, "Generally people with the highest status in society are the most likely to go to the polls." Thus, older Americans, homeowners, married couples and people with higher edu-cation and income represent the bulk of U.S. voters.

While Hispanics are gaining in homeownership and have family values that support marriage, they remain the youngest and least educated of all groups, and generally have the lowest income. Further, when voting figures for Hispanics are compared with the total Hispanic population – that includes non-voting immigrants – the percentage of voting among Hispanics is not very impressive. When only voting-eligible Hispanics are compared to those who actually vote, the percentage increases by 20 points according to the Census Bureau.

Perhaps the most significant effect of Hispanic voting trends is yet to come. As the Hispanic population ages, becomes more educated, has a better income, buys more homes and has additional disposable income to fund political activity, a powerful political force will be truly realized. If demographic projections hold true, Hispanic voters will increasingly influence each presidential election for the next 50 years.

Hispanic voting patterns with regard to the two main political parties represent a bit of a puzzle. The number of Hispanics voting the Republican ticket during the 1998 midterm elections increased slightly. But because of the GOP's reputation for supporting curbs on immigration and attempting to abolish affirmative action,[18] Hispanics, including many CEOs, have tended to vote the Democratic ticket, even if they considered themselves conservative. Further, Hispanics believe Republicans' efforts to dismantle affirmative action nationwide will continue.[19] Yet, Governor Bush received tremendous support from Hispanics in one of the mega states, Texas. Jed Bush in Florida also seems to have strong Hispanic support.

The Democratic Party has traditionally received a larger share of the Hispanic vote, and there is a strong possibility that Hispanics will continue to support the Democrats in the 2000 elections. The Clinton administration's small number of Hispanic appointees, approximately 5 percent, sends Hispanic leaders the message that Democrats take them for granted. Yet most California Hispanics seem to support the Democratic ticket and the same is likely in New York. The national elections in 2000 will provide an update on the voting preferences of Hispanics.

The Characteristics of Hispanics

Purchasing power, wealth creation and economic empowerment are placing Hispanics in the center of a social and cultural revolution. But who are Hispanics? What defines them, and what underlying demographic trends have highlighted the progress made by this diverse community? What are the challenges and how could these affect many Americans?

The Spanish language and allegiance to family are key to understanding the Hispanic experience in the United States. Spanish defines Hispanics and plays an important role in their increased purchasing power. The focus on family bonds, also a defining characteristic, is helping move Hispanics into the middle class. Although Hispanic communities are richly diverse, they share strong ties. The emotional connections of language, ethnic pride and common values include a tremendously strong bond of sharing a homeland within the United States. This is the definitive common denominator for Hispanics.

We, The American Hispanics, a 1993 report by the U.S. Department of Commerce, describes Hispanics this way: "We trace our origin or descent to Spain or to Mexico, Puerto Rico, Cuba and many other Spanish-speaking countries of Latin America."[20]

The words "Hispanics" and "Latinos" are debated as inappropriate names for a broad range of peoples with distinct cultures. The issue is a sore spot among those who see Hispanics as neither a race nor an ethnic group. Neither descriptor is fully accepted because each is based on place of origin – Hispanics from the Iberian Peninsula and Latinos from Latin or romance languages. The terms are used interchangeably because discussions of self-definition have not produced a better alternative. So, rather than getting caught up in the controversy, we will describe the characteristics that tie these communities together while noting the diversity that exists among them.

Spanish and English

The Spanish language is the cultural characteristic that unites Hispanics. No wonder that debates about bilingual education often have personal as well as pedagogical and political overtones. Hispanics often choose to speak two languages – a practical option that honors identity and integration and is quickly becoming a commodity for the community as globalization continues to increase.

The 1990 census information on language use at home reflects this, and the 2000 census is likely to confirm it. Bicultural Hispanics represent about 54 percent of the Hispanic population. Forty-six percent of Hispanics speak Spanish and English "very well," and another 20 percent say they speak Spanish and English "well." Considering the large number of predominantly Spanish-speaking immigrants entering the United States each year, these figures represent a positive trend.

Charles Gonzales makes the case clearly. "The Spanish language is a tie that binds us all together. But these days, it is a global tie. More people now speak Spanish worldwide than any other language. Our language skills and comfort in dealing with Latino culture allow us to take advantage of global economic trends." He concludes, "Spanish has moved out of the barrios and into the boardrooms."[21]

Miami is a good example of the increasing demand for fully bilingual employees in U.S. cities – those who speak, read and write English and Spanish fluently. Businesses in the city manage about 30 percent of all U.S. trade with South America and 43 percent of trade with Central America.[22] In addition, some 130 international corporations opened offices in South Florida in 1998, making the demand for fully bilingual employees high in Miami.

City leaders fear the shortage of bilingual employees will damage and could eventually "throttle" the city's economy. Thus, with the help of the Greater Miami Chamber of Commerce, business executives have launched a campaign to educate parents and youth about the importance of becoming fully literate in both languages.

The case of Visa International shows how this shortage affects businesses. Most of its 300 South Florida employees must communicate with about 700 Latin American banks. Because it is difficult finding fully bilingual employees, Visa now offers a Spanish-language training program to all its employees, Hispanic and non-Hispanic.

Being multilingual in a global economy follows the law of supply and demand. If the use of two languages is an economic advantage for Hispanics, then the debate over bilingual education should move to a different level. Perhaps it should focus on the number of languages all children, not just Hispanics, should study to be prepared to participate in the global economy.

The Hispanic Family

Even more important to Hispanics than the Spanish language are their families, which tend to be larger than the average American family. Census figures from 1990 show most Hispanics lived with their families and had the lowest divorce rate in the United States. About 70 percent of Hispanic households were maintained by married couples, about 22 percent by a female with no husband present and about 8 percent by a male with no wife present.

The migration into middle class and homeownership, according to Gregory Rodriguez is due to family members working together. For example, in order to afford a home of their own, it is not uncommon for a lower-income family to have three or four sources of income, which they pool – the parents working several jobs and the children both working and attending school. Also, immigrant families who may not have a college graduate among them, and therefore have lower salaries, purchase many new homes.

The Ramos family of Los Angeles is an example of this trend.[23] Humberto, the oldest of 10 children, recalls that when he was growing up:

> We all pitched in. We would go to school, be out by 3 p.m. … and had an early dinner. Then we worked with my dad, cutting people's yards. We came home, took a shower, and said the Rosary. We went to bed, got up at 5 in the morning to do our homework. Dad would go to work at 2 a.m. because he was also a janitor at a supermarket. He would be out by 11:00 a.m. He'd come home, sleep for a couple of hours and wait for us to come home. Then we would start all over again.

His father and mother both came to the U.S. illegally, purchased rental property as well as their own home and put all 10 children through college.

The downside of resource pooling is that a college education may be postponed or abandoned to keep the family's head above water. An investment in education means additional expenses and less money in the pot. This is especially true in families where the children earn a little over minimum wage and bring home more money than their parents. The trend to favor work over education is so prevalent that some Hispanic leaders have developed special programs to teach parents the importance of a college education to the family's future income.

Demographic Characteristics

Articles now appear more and more often in the popular and business literature detailing the tremendous growth of the U.S. Hispanic population. Unless otherwise noted, the following figures came from the Census Bureau's *Hispanic Heritage Month 1999: September 15-October 15 Facts for Features* CB99-FF.12, distributed on September 13, 1999; *We, the*

American Hispanics, September 1993; or directly from the Department of Commerce's U.S. Bureau of the Census Web site.

Population Distribution and Growth Projections

In 1990, there were 22.4 million Hispanics in the United States, almost 9 percent of the nation's population. That was 53 percent higher than the 1980 figure. Yet, Hispanics may have been undercounted by as much as 5 percent, according to the Census Bureau, which estimates that in California alone, about 1 million people were not counted.[24]

Between April 1, 1990, and June 1, 1999, the nation's resident Hispanic population increased by 8.9 million to an estimated 31.3 million, surpassing the population of Canada at 30 million. This figure, representing 11.5 percent of the total U.S. population, does not include an estimated 3.9 million persons living in Puerto Rico as of July 1, 1998.

In total, this makes the U.S. Hispanic population the fifth largest Latino population in the world, smaller only than the populations of Mexico, Spain, Colombia and Argentina. In terms of consumption, U.S. Hispanics have the largest discretionary income of all Spanish-speaking groups, making the U.S. Hispanic market one of the more promising emerging markets in the world.[25]

According to *Hispanic Magazine*,[26] the U.S. Latino population grew at a rate six times faster than the general population between 1990 and 1996 and was expected to reach 35 million by the year 2000. Between April 1, 1990 and June 1, 1999, the resident Hispanic population accounted for an estimated 37.2 percent of the nation's resident population growth.

Projections by the U.S. Census Bureau show that Hispanic Americans will form the largest minority group in the United

States by the year 2005. Indeed, Hispanic children under 18 already form the largest minority in their age group, according to the National Center for Health Statistics.[27] By 2020, Hispanics will make up 20 percent of U.S. youth.

This growth rate is likely to continue. The Census Bureau's 1992 middle series projection, an interim census, suggests rapid growth may continue into the 21st century. Thus, the Hispanic population could rise to 52.7 million or 16 percent of the total U.S. population by 2020, 59 million by 2030 and 81 million by 2050, when one in every five U.S. residents will be of Hispanic origin.

Most of this growth will come from U.S.-born Hispanics. Despite the dramatic increase in immigration among Hispanics – as an example 70 percent of Hispanics who entered the United States between 1980 and 1990 were from Central America alone, a dramatic increase over the 20 percent who arrived between 1970 and 1979 – they remain a minority among Hispanics. A little over one-third of the Hispanics in this country are foreign-born.

Distribution by State

The Hispanic market has experienced tremendous growth in all states. As of July 1, 1998, seven states had Hispanic populations of at least 1 million: California had 10.1 million; Texas, 5.9 million; New York, 2.6 million; Florida, 2.2 million; Illinois, 1.2 million; and New Jersey and Arizona, 1 million each. Together, California and Texas are home to more than half of the nation's Hispanics. In 1990, nearly nine of every 10 Hispanics lived in just 10 states, including those mentioned above as well as New Mexico, Colorado and Massachusetts.

The Magic Four

Age, education, employment and income – the magic four – are closely related demographic indicators. Hispanics will become both the largest and the youngest minority in the United States in 2005[28] and will have the lowest level of education. While each Hispanic group shows unique trends in rate of growth, average ages and educational levels, groups with the youngest representation have the least amount of education and wealth. Thus, despite the tremendous purchasing power of Hispanics, there are weak points in the pipeline that must be addressed by both Hispanic and non-Hispanic U.S. leaders.

Age

Nearly 40 percent of the Hispanic population was under 20 years of age in 1990, compared with 28 percent of the non-Hispanic population.[29] Hispanics have a higher proportion of young adults and children and fewer elderly than the non-Hispanic population. In 1990, nearly seven of every 10 Hispanics were younger than 35 years, compared with just five of every 10 non-Hispanics. Only about 5 percent of Hispanics were 65 years and older, compared with 13 percent of non-Hispanics.

The U.S. median age is 34 compared to 24 for Mexican-Americans. Cubans are the oldest of all Hispanic communities with a median age of 39.

Hispanics will require products, services and resources for young families, at a time when the majority population is requiring products, services and resources for older adults. It may be that Hispanics and the rest of the American population are competing for resources or it may be that by investing in these young families, the older Americans will benefit through the contribution to taxes and Social Security.

Leaders in social policy will have the challenge of proposing and producing the latter win-win situation.

Education

Education is the surest road to success in the United States. This is why Hispanics' low but improving college graduation rates and high but decreasing dropout rates are so significant. In many ways the country's future is inexorably linked to the educational progress of Hispanic Americans. They will account for 25 percent of the total school population by 2030, according to Laura I. Rendon.[30]

By 2006, a shortage of 3.3 million workers with college-level skills is expected in such growth areas as management, professional technical areas, health care and education – jobs that Hispanics will need to fill if the nation is to continue to prosper. According to Patricia Guadalupe of *Hispanic Business*, when most baby boomers reach retirement age, Hispanics will constitute one fifth of U.S. workers.[31] Thus, education issues affecting Hispanics are not just a Hispanic concern, according to Selena Walsh, director of policy and communications for LULAC.[32] A well-educated and marketable Hispanic work force will fill essential U.S. jobs, contribute to Social Security and pay taxes at a time when it will be most needed given the large number of retiring adults in the overall population.

The good news is that more Hispanics are graduating from high school. In 1997, 62 percent earned a high school diploma, up from 53 percent in 1994. Over the last 20 years, college enrollment by Hispanics has tripled, hitting 1.1 million in 1995. At least another 500,000 Hispanics between the ages of 18 and 24 are expected to be in college by 2015.

The bad news is that the Hispanic high school dropout rate at 28 percent is twice that of African-Americans and more than three times that of Anglos. When they graduate from high school, Hispanics often have college preparation deficiencies: lower grade-point averages and lower admissions test scores than the other groups. This gap can preclude college eligibility. Consequently, about 57 percent of Hispanic undergraduates enroll at community colleges.

According to Sara Martinez Tucker, president of the Hispanic Scholarship Fund, low graduation rates and low representation in higher education have lifelong consequences because they lead to overrepresentation in service jobs and lower median incomes. Lower family income often determines whether a child can be sent to college.[33] For example, Raul Yzaguirre, chairman and CEO of the National Council of La Raza, notes that three out of 10 Hispanic students drop out of school due to inequities in school financing. School districts with high concentrations of Latino students are less likely than those with low or no Latino populations to have adequate funding, according to Aida Alvarez, administrator of the Small Business Administration.[34]

Sara Martinez Tucker reports that lack of financial resources is the primary reason Hispanic students give for not attending college.[35] Laws that affect education, such as the affirmative action decisions in California and Texas, present further problems. While opposing views exist within the Hispanic community, the weight of opinion is that these initiatives negatively affect Hispanics, and many are willing to take a political stand in this area. This was most clearly seen in the 1996 gubernatorial elections in California, when Democratic candidate Gray Davis received the majority of Hispanic votes after Republican Governor Pete Wilson supported Proposition 209, which banned racial preferences in hiring and education.

Nevertheless, Hispanics have made great strides in higher education since the 1970s. The number of Latinos graduating from college has tripled during the last 20 years.[36] In 1970, only one Hispanic in 20 completed four or more years of college compared to one in 10 in 1996, according to the 15th annual status report from the Minorities in Higher Education. However, this figure falls significantly short of the one-in-four figure for non-Hispanic whites of the same age.[37]

A comparison of data between 1977 and 1993 showed progressive improvements in numbers of Hispanics who attained bachelor's and master's degrees.

First professional degrees, a designation of the Census Bureau for medicine, law, and engineering, showed the largest increase. In 1977, 2 percent of Hispanics had bachelor's degrees. By 1993 that figure was 3.9 percent. The number of master's degrees showed a similar rise. In 1977, 1.9 percent had master's degrees, up to 2.9 percent by 1993. First professionals showed the highest increase, from 1.7 percent in 1977 to 4 percent in 1993. In 2000, the number of Hispanics earning bachelor's and master's degrees were expected to surpass 99,000 and 21,700, respectively. That's more than triple the numbers from 1979 – 30,000 and 6,500, according to HispanTelligence.[38]

Business is the fastest growing field of study among Hispanic college students, according to the American Council on Education.[39] The number of Hispanic students earning bachelor's degrees in business increased 228 percent between 1977 and 1993, when approximately 20 percent of Hispanic undergraduates were pursuing business degrees. Master's degrees in business administration increased 346 percent.

Employment

Access to well-paying jobs is key to increasing purchasing power. Hispanics' disproportionately high representation among the unemployed and in low-paying service jobs lessens their potential purchasing power. According to a 1998 report by the U.S. Department of Labor, unemployment rates for Latinos dropped from 11.3 percent in January 1993 to 7.5 percent in August 1998[40] when the national unemployment rate stood at 4.5 percent.

In addition, Hispanics rarely fill upper-management jobs in either the federal government or in Fortune 1000 firms. The 1999 *Hispanic Business* corporate elite directory[41] includes 356 Hispanic executives at the level of vice president or higher at 144 Fortune 1000 companies. This is a gain of 79 executives, or 28 percent, from the 1998 list, but a tiny improvement compared with the total number of senior-level professionals.[42]

In October 1998, the U.S. Office of Personnel Management announced a new 10-point plan to recruit more Hispanics into federal government. At the time, Hispanics constituted only 193 of the 5,238 workers at the Senior Executive Service (SES) level in the federal government, where budgetary and procurement decisions are made.[43]

Between 1980 and 1997, the number of Hispanics in managerial and professional specialty occupations tripled from 670,000 to 1.8 million, growing annually by an average of 6 percent. HispanTelligence predicts that in 2020, 16.8 percent of the U.S. Hispanic population will be part of the professional and managerial ranks.[44]

According to *Hispanic Business*, more Hispanics who are employed are finding jobs in the labor and service sectors. While Hispanics employed in the service industry grew to 20.2 percent of the general Hispanic population in 1997, compared with 16.3 percent in 1980, their numbers in the operator, fabricator and laborer sector constituted 22.7 percent of the general population, down from 28.4 percent in 1980. An increase in the number of Hispanics assuming corporate leadership positions may account for this shift.

The figures for Latinas significantly lead the overall statistics. A study by the AFL-CIO Working Woman's Department from the survey "Ask a Working Woman" revealed that in 1998, less than 1 percent of working Latinas earned more than $75,000 a year. Furthermore, 82 percent of Latinas earned less than $25,000 a year.[45]

However, in recent years, Hispanic women have addressed this issue squarely. With limited corporate options, they are venturing out in record numbers to start and grow their own companies. Thus they form the fastest growing group of business owners in the country, according to a U.S. Census Bureau study. The businesses they own increased by 206 percent between 1987 and 1996, according to the National Foundation for Women Business Owners. Marisa Rivera-Albert, president of the National Hispana Leadership Institute in Washington, D.C., a nonprofit enterprise that works to develop Hispanic women as ethical world leaders, comments, "If corporate America doesn't embrace them more rewardingly, Latinas will continue leaving corporate jobs to start their own businesses."[46] Thus, starting a business is a life decision that offers Hispanic women better options.

Income

As mentioned, age, education and types of jobs have a direct impact on income. While the trend looks positive, compared with the rest of America, Hispanics have ground to gain. According to the Census Bureau, Hispanic households' real or inflation-adjusted median income increased by 4.5 percent between 1996 and 1997, when annual incomes averaged $25,477 and $26,628, respectively. By comparison, real per capita income rose 4.8 percent, from $10,279 to $10,773.

In the same period, the number of Hispanic poor decreased from 8.7 million to 8.3 million, and the overall poverty rate decreased from 29.4 percent to 24.7 percent. While the U.S. consumer market has grown significantly in recent years, poverty rates for Hispanics remain stubbornly high. Just over 20 percent of families were living in poverty in 1990 compared with less than 10 percent of non-Hispanic families. Approximately 27 percent of Hispanics are classified as poor, compared with 11 percent for non-Hispanics.

In 1990, the median family income for Hispanics was $25,064, compared with $35,225 for all American families. Six years later, that gap had narrowed. Barbara Robles, an associate professor at the University of Texas in Austin, comments, "The picture looks better, but is not yet rosy. The 1996 Hispanic per capita income is $8,000 lower than the per capita income for all races."[47]

There are some distressing trends. The proportion of Hispanics earning between $25,000 and $75,000 annually fell from 47.2 percent to 43.8 percent between 1980 and 1997. This appears to parallel a national trend[48] and may also be influenced by the recent influx of immigrants. Even more disturbing, inflation-adjusted per capita income for Hispanics grew at an annual rate of just 0.7 percent between 1980 and 1997, compared with a 1.4 percent increase for Anglos and 1.6 percent for African-Americans. The gap grew especially wide during the 1990s, when the rate of growth in Hispanic income was roughly half that of the nation as a whole. Hispanic per capita income reached $10,773 in 1997, just 56 percent of that for the general population and 53 percent of that for Anglos.

Summary

The Hispanic community – through its purchasing power, wealth creation and political empowerment – is changing the American culture in very significant ways, from pop culture to economics. Now 35 million strong and growing, Hispanics will become the largest and youngest minority in the United States in 2005.

But, positive trends in education, jobs and income also have weak patches that will most likely affect all Americans, since Hispanics will make up one-fifth of the employees paying into Social Security at the time when aging baby boomers retire. Hispanic movement out of poverty into middle-class status and home ownership has its roots in family values of pooling resources, education and entrepreneurship. Hispanic affluence is squarely rooted in entrepreneurship. Over 50 percent of the people on the Hispanic Rich List reported by *Hispanic Business* acquired or grew their wealth through business ownership.[49] Thus, Hispanics and entrepreneurship are playing an important role today and in the future of the United States.

Notes

[1]Charles Gonzalez, J. Reichert, and P. Caldwell, *Yes you Can! Every Latino's Guide to Building Family Wealth* (Worchester, Massachusetts: Chandler House Press, 1998), 4.

[2]Jeffrey M. Humphreys, "Hispanic buying power by place of residence: 1990-1999," *Georgia Business and Economic Conditions* (1998) November-December.

[3]NCLR, *Education, work, and economic well-being*, (www.nclr.or/about/fqa-latino.html#2, 2000).

[4]Humphreys.

[5]U.S.Census Bureau, U.S. International trade statistics, (www.census.gov/ftp/pub/foreign-trade/www, 2000) March 16.

[6]Anna Escobedo-Cabral, *The president's message*, The Hispanic Association on Corporate Responsibility. www.hacr.org (2000).

[7]Joel Russell, "The $25 million dollar question," *Hispanic Business* (2000) March, 14-16.

[8]Gonzalez, et al, 4.

[9]Gonzalez, et al, 6.

[10]Gregory Rodriguez, *The emerging Latino middle class* (Pepperdine University Institute for Public Policy, 1996).

[11]Robert D. Cruz, "Parity on payday?" *Hispanic Business* (1999) April, 36.

[12]*Hispanic Business*, "The state of the Hispanic economy." *Hispanic Business* (1999) April, 22.

[13]Rodriguez.

[14]Univision Communication, Inc., *Hispanic voters: A new force* (*www.univision.net/hispanicvoters/5.html*, 1999).

[15]Juan Andrade, Jr., "Latinos: A sleeping giant?" *Hispanic* (1998) June, 54

[16]Patricia Guadalupe, "Vying for votes," *Hispanic Business* (1998) March, 94

[17]Lynne M. Casper and L. Bass, *Voting and registration in the election of November 1999* (U.S. Census Bureau. www.census.gov/population/www/socdemo/voting/vote-htabtcon.html, 1999).

[18]Russell.

[19]Rick Mendosa, "One happy CEO," *Hispanic Business* (1997) December, 19-20.

[20]*We the American Hispanics*, U.S. Census Bureau (1998), 1.

[21]Gonzalez, et al, 4.

[22]Dereck Reveron, "Spanlish won't count cut it," *Hispanic Business* (1998) November, 14-16.

[23]*Parade Magazine* (1999) January, 3-6.

[24]Joel Russell, "High profile progress," *Hispanic Business* (1998) December, 66-68.

[25]Cruz, 36.

[26]Robert Famigheti, ed., "World population," *The World Almanac and Book of Facts* (World Almanac Books, 2000).

[27]The National Center for Health Statistics, "America's Children: Key national indicators of well-being – Part I: Population & family characteristics," *Federal Interagency Forum on Child and Family Statistics* (www.childstats.gov, 1999).

[28]Maria Zate, "The tomorrow question," *Hispanic Business* (1997) October, 40-42.

[29]Zate.

[30]*Hispanic Business*, "Upward mobility," Hispanic Business (1999) April, 28-30.

[31]Patricia Guadalupe, "Reaching to Hispanics," *Hispanic Business* (1999) October, 16.

[32]*Hispanic Business*, "LULAC marks 70 years," *Hispanic Business*. April, 18.

[33]Zate.

[34]Aida Alvarez, U.S. Small Business Administration, addressing the White House Initiative on educational excellence for Hispanic Americans/AVANCE Conference, *SBA Speeches*. (1998) October, 6.

[35]Jonathan J. Higuera, "Hitting the jackpot," *Hispanic Business* (1999) September, 64-66.

[36]Andrade.

[37] Deborah Carter and Reginald Wilson, "Status report on minorities in higher education,"*American Council on Education* (ACE), Fifteenth annual report, Office of Minorities in Higher Education (OMHE) (1996).

[38] *Hispanic Business*, "Upward mobility."

[39] American Council on Education, Minorities in Higher Education – Minority Markets Alert, "Education? Si! More Hispanics enroll in college; business is their concentration," *EMP Communications, Inc.* (1996) October.

[40] *Hispanic* "Facts and figures," *Hispanic*. (1999) April, 17.

[41] *Hispanic Business*, "The 1999 corporate elite directory: The annual tally of top managers," *Hispanic Business* (1999) January-February, 22-40

[42] *Hispanic Business*, "Upward mobility."

[43] Guadalupe, 8.

[44] *Hispanic Business*, "Upward mobility."

[45] AFL-CIO, "It's time for working women to earn equal pay," *AFL-CIO Ask a working woman survey*. (www.aflcio.org/home.htm, 2000)

[46] Christine Granados, "Corporate exodus," *Hispanic* (1999) July/August, 50-54.

[47] Nick Douglas, "Strong economy buoys purchasing power," *Hispanic Business* (1997) December, 58.

[48] Constance Mitchell-Ford and P.Barta, "Income gap broadens amid boom," *The Wall Street Journal* (2000) January 18, A2.

[49] Russell, "The $25 million question."

CHAPTER THREE

BUSINESS DEMOGRAPHICS AND TRENDS

The history of Hispanic enterprise in the New World has deep roots. After all, Cristóbal Colón, the "CEO" of a trade expedition, came this way in 1492 looking for a route to ship spices from the East Indies to Spain. Isabella and Ferdinand, the Spanish monarchs, financed him in a deal that would have been ideal by any venture capitalist's standard.

As early as 1614, 11 years before the Pilgrims landed at Plymouth Rock, Native Americans joined Spanish explorers to form families that settled what is today Santa Fe, New Mexico, beginning the story of Hispanic entrepreneurs in America.

In his book *Hispanic Firsts: 500 Years of Extraordinary Achievement*,[1] Nicolás Kanellos traces the story of these early business ventures. In 1598, Juan de Oñate introduced livestock breeding to the Southwest. Livestock ranching subsequently developed quickly into huge estates in the Spanish colonies and became the basis of wealth among early Hispanic Americans.

In 1690, Captain Alonso de León brought the first cattle to the Spanish mission known as San Francisco de las Tejas, opening the cattle industry in East Texas. In 1760, Captain

Blas María de la Garza Falcón started what later became the largest cattle ranch in the Americas – the King Ranch of Texas. Further, in the Southeast, Tomás Menéndez Márquez built the largest cattle ranch in Florida and developed an early trading business with Spanish-settled Cuba. In 1763, Francisco Javier Sánchez became the first native-born Hispanic American to achieve large-scale success as a merchant and entrepreneur.

Early on women entrepreneurs also played important roles.[2] María Hinojosa de Bali became Texas' first cattle queen, controlling over one third of the present Rio Grande Valley. Patricia de la Garza de León helped found the city of Victoria, Texas, and became one of the richest women in the state. Further, one of the first women entrepreneurs on the American frontier, María Gertrudes Barceló, began her first gaming business in 1825 and later opened the Wild West's first gambling casinos in Santa Fe.

According to Kanellos:

> The Treaty of Guadalupe Hidalgo in 1848, which ended the Mexican-American war, created 80,000 new U.S. Hispanic citizens overnight, some of Mexican origin and others of Spanish origin. This ended the Spanish rule in this part of the New World, which had lasted 330 years. When this treaty took effect, Hispanic pioneers had already established economically flourishing cities and states: San Francisco, San Diego, Los Angeles, San Bernardino, San Antonio, Santa Fe, St. Augustine, Colorado, Texas, Florida, California and Montana.

Hispanic entrepreneurship has a strong heritage in both the early pioneering Hispanics and Hispanic immigrant communities. The flourishing of these communities today marks the rise of a striking Hispanic economic renaissance.

Hispanic Business Demographics

The U.S. Department of Commerce conducts its economic census every five years, leading to reports that are released two years later. The latest available economic census data are for 1992. As part of this census, the Survey of Minority-Owned Business Enterprises (SMOBE) generates reports for each minority group. Some organizations, including the Small Business Administration (SBA), have produced studies based on census data that project figures beyond 1992 for specific states or areas. These reports suggest that, overall, Hispanic businesses have experienced a significant growth in numbers, have higher receipts, employ more people than ever before, and have increased their payrolls. Most Hispanic businesses are located in three states and are concentrated in business services industries. Finally, most are sole proprietorships or subchapter "S" corporations. Latina businesses lead the charge significantly skewing the statistics for Hispanic businesses; and finally, international trade is a growth area for many Hispanic business owners.

Number of Firms

The SBA and the U.S. Hispanic Chamber of Commerce estimate that Hispanics owned from 1.4 million to 1.5 million businesses in 1997.[3] According to the economic census, the number of Hispanic businesses have grown significantly since 1987, approximately 306 percent in the 10 years from 1987 to 1997. During that same period, the number of all U.S. companies grew by 26 percent, from 13.7 million to 17.3 million. In 1992, 4.3 percent of all U.S. companies were Hispanic-owned, in 1997 about 5 percent. Table 1 shows the growth in numbers of Hispanic-owned firms from 1987 and projected through 2020.

Table 1: Growth in Number of Hispanic-Owned Firms				
1987	1992	1997	2000	Projected for 2020
489,973	862,605	1.4 to 1.5M	1.5 to 2M	3.3

Aida Alvarez, head of the SBA, suggests that the 83 percent growth rate in the five-year period between 1987 and 1992 is extraordinary, "Hispanics are creating businesses three times faster than the general population. This tremendous growth rate for the last 10 years is in large part due to the proliferation of Latina businesses." This is the fastest growing entrepreneurial group in the American business community.[4]

According to *Hispanic* magazine, if projections hold true, by the end of 2000 there should be more than two million Hispanic businesses.[5] Conservative projections see that number increasing to 3.3 million over the next 20 years.[6] These estimates, impressive on their own, do not include the highly successful Hispanic-owned companies that merge with mainstream companies and lose their minority status, or the mature and larger Hispanic "C" corporations which the census does not track.

Hispanics represent about 11 percent of the population and only 5 percent of the businesses. The Hispanic business community has a way to go to reach parity with their proportion within the general population. Yet, the numbers of businesses for 2000 are probably much higher than the projected two million Hispanic-owned firms, and the potential remains great for continued growth.

Receipts

The SBA estimates that in 1997 (the most recent figures), Hispanic-owned businesses generated receipts of $184 billion, representing a 400 percent increase in revenues from 1987. The U.S. Hispanic Chamber of Commerce estimates that in 1999, Hispanic-owned companies generated more than $200 billion in revenues.[7] *Hispanic Business* estimates revenues from these firms will reach $221 billion by the end of 2000 and $336 billion by 2020.[8]

According to a recent SBA report,[9] the 5 percent of all firms representing Hispanic-owned firms took in 2.3 percent of gross receipts in 1992.[10] Table 2 shows the tremendous difference in receipts and percentage growth between Hispanic and all U.S. firms.

Table 2: Receipts and Percent Growth between 1987 and 1992 for Hispanic and All American Firms			
Firms	1987 Receipts	1992 Receipts	% Growth
Hispanic	32.8 billion	76.8 billion	234%
All U.S.	2 trillion	3.3 trillion	67%

Hispanic-owned companies tended to be smaller in size than the average U.S. company and took in much less revenue: $94,000 per business, compared with $193,000 per business nationwide.

Payroll and Employment

Payrolls at Hispanic businesses grew by $7.6 billion between 1987 and 1992, a 232 percent increase.[11] Total employment went from 264,846 in 1987 to 691,056 in 1992, a 383 percent increase. *Hispanic Business* magazine adds that Hispanic-owned companies are expected to employ 1.5 million workers by the end of the year 2000. That is projected to grow to 2.5 million by 2020.[12]

Minority Group Comparison

Hispanic businesses were the most numerous minority-owned enterprises by 1997, accounting for 1.4 million of the 3.25 million total.[13] Table 3 shows the minority firm comparison.

Table 3: Minority Firm Comparison			
Minority Firms	Number	% Growth 1987 to 1997	% Revenue After Inflation 1987 to 1997
Hispanic	1.4 million	232%	417 %
Asian	1.1 million	180%	463%
African American	880,000	180%	109%

Nearly one quarter of Asian-owned business, one seventh of Hispanic-owned businesses and one tenth of black-owned businesses had employees.

Hispanic Subgroup Ownership

In 1992, Mexican-Americans owned 49.1 percent of all Hispanic businesses and had 39.7 percent of total receipts. Central and South Americans owned 20.9 percent of the businesses and had 16.6 percent receipts. Cubans owned 12.1 percent of the firms and had 21.4 percent of receipts. Puerto Ricans owned 6.1 percent and had 5.2 percent of receipts. Other Hispanics owned 6.0 percent and had 8.6 percent of receipts. Spanish-Americans owned 5.9 percent of all Hispanic firms and had 8.5 percent of receipts.

States and Top Metropolitan Areas

According to the economic census, three states – California, Texas and Florida, where 61 percent of the nation's Hispanic population lives – accounted for 68 percent of the companies owned by Hispanics in 1992. California had 132,212; Texas, 94,754; and Florida, 64,413. Additionally, New York had 28,254; New Mexico 21,586; Illinois, 18,368; Arizona, 12,835; and Colorado, 13,817.

Table 4 shows the number, percent of total businesses in the state and the percent of total receipts for the state in the top five metropolitan areas.

Table 4: Top Five Metropolitan Areas for Hispanic-Owned Businesses			
Metro Areas	Number	Percent of Total in State	Percent of Total Receipts
LA/LongBeach	108,104	16.4	5.3
Miami	77,300	47.8	30.06
New York City	39,175	7.3	1.7
Houston	33,765	12.9	3.6
Riverside/ San Bernandino, California	21,380	13.1	5.9

Industries

The 1992 SMOBE report showed that 45 percent of Hispanic-owned firms were in the service industries, which took in 23 percent of total receipts. More than half of those firms were concentrated in the areas of business and personal services, the majority in business services. This is borne out by the marked increase in degrees for first professionals – doctors, lawyers and engineers.

While the service sector comprised the most firms, sales were highest in retail trade, which made up just 14 percent of the firms but took in 24 percent of total receipts. Automotive dealers and gasoline service stations, eating and drinking establishments and food stores made up 40 percent of all retail trade companies but generated 72 percent of the receipts.

In 1987, 43.7 percent of all Hispanic-owned firms were in the service industries.[14] The strongest relative growth, both in numbers and receipts, was in wholesale trade and manufacturing. The number of businesses in the wholesale trade industry rose by 202 percent, from 3,359 in 1982 to 10,154 in 1987. Receipts grew by 219 percent, from $766.65 million in 1982 to $2.45 billion in 1987.

Legal Structure

The legal structure used most often by Hispanic businesses closely mirrors the national norm for small businesses – the majority are sole proprietorships followed by subchapter "S" corporations. The 1992 census showed 89.3 percent or 689,0015 Hispanic firms were sole proprietorships, compared with 93.9 percent, or 396,769, in the 1987 census. This decrease in percentages occurred despite the dramatic increase in numbers of firms. Interestingly, the proportion of gross receipts taken in by sole proprietorships decreased substantially, from 61.3 percent in 1987 to 35.3 percent in 1992.

The considerable increase in numbers of businesses using the next most common legal structure might suggest a maturing of businesses since the 1987 census, or perhaps an influx of new entrepreneurs more interested in a corporate structure. In 1992, 6.5 percent of the Hispanic firms reported were subchapter "S" corporations and accounted for 48.4 percent of gross receipts. That was up from 3.2 percent of firms and 29.4 percent of gross receipts in 1987. The number of partnerships also increased, from 12,230 or 2.9 percent in 1987 to 4.2 percent in 1992. Partnerships represented 16.4 percent of gross receipts in 1992.

Business Trends

Amid the tremendous growth of Hispanic-owned businesses, two trends stand out: Latinas are starting and growing businesses faster than other business sectors, and Hispanic entrepreneurs are actively participating in international trade.

Latina-Owned Businesses

From 1987 to 1996, the number of Latina-owned firms grew in number by 206 percent, according to the National Foundation for Women Business Owners (NFWBO), a non-profit research organization affiliated with the National Association for Women Business Owners.[15] This rate of growth is nearly four times that of the general business population[16] at 47 percent.

Sharon Hadary, executive director of NFWBO, commented:

No group came close in growth rates, particularly in traditionally male-dominated fields: The number of Latina firms rose 428 percent in construction, 389 percent in agriculture and 338 percent in wholesale trade. Overall sales by Latina-owned enterprises grew by 534 percent and employment jumped 487 percent. Growth is only the beginning. It's not only that we have more [Latina-owned] firms; they're larger, more sophisticated and making a greater contribution to our economy.[17]

NFWBO projected there were 383,400 Latina-owned firms in 1996. Latina-owned businesses make up 35 percent of all minority women-owned businesses, 5 percent of all women-owned firms and 15 percent of all minority-owned firms. NFWBO projected in 1997 that Latinas owned more than 33 percent of Hispanic firms, employed 31 percent of their workers and generated 25 percent of the sales.[18]

Revenues and employment also showed marked increases according to NFWBO. Between 1987 and 1996, sales generated by Latina-owned firms rose by 534 percent to $63.7 billion, while employment increased by 206 percent to 671,200. This tremendous growth reflects the trend for women entrepreneurs in general. The 7.95 million women-owned businesses employed 18.5 million people and generated close to $2.3 trillion in sales in 1996.

Latina entrepreneurs credit their success to an increase in the number of Latina role models, changing gender roles, business loan programs for women and a dramatic change in cultural values supporting women in leadership positions. The increasing influence of Latinas is strong, as is their bond to family and community. Besides the opportunity to exercise leadership, Latinas believe that entrepreneurship allows them the flexibility to balance or integrate business, family and community.

Considering the increased challenges and opportunities for leadership, higher income and greater flexibility, entrepreneurship provides Latinas an attractive option. A study by Catalyst,[19] a nonprofit research and advisory organization, called *Women of Color in Corporate Management: A Statistical Picture*,[20] found that Latinas are underrepresented in management positions, on corporate boards and in executive positions, as are all women. Further, the report found that Latinas have the lowest median income of any women's minority group. By comparison, Latinas earned $423 per week; African-American women, $514; and Asian women, $593.

For every dollar white male managers make, white women managers make 59 cents, and women of color earn an average of two cents less. *Ask a Working Woman*, a study by the AFL-CIO, also looked at the income of Latinas.[21] It found that less than 1 percent of working Latinas earned more than $75,000 a year in 1998, and 82 percent earned less than $25,000 a year. It is not surprising that Latinas are breaking records in seeking business ownership and growth.

Latinas are on the rise in other areas as well. The number elected to public office has risen 400 percent since 1984, more than four times the rate for Latinos overall, according to the National Association of Latino Elected and Appointed Officials (NALEO).[22] Further, more Latinas are in leadership positions in traditionally male-led Hispanic organizations. For example, the U.S. Hispanic Chamber of Commerce counts seven Latinas among its 24-member board of directors. Four Latinas serve on the Latin Business Association's 15-member board, and the Texas Association of Mexican-American Chambers of Commerce (TAMACC) has its first Latina chairperson, Marilu Martínez Stevens, in its 24 years of existence.

Latinas continue to show progress in other areas but also have challenges to address. In 1996, 25 percent of college-age Latinas had some college credits. Between 1973 and 1996, the number of Latinas earning bachelor's degrees increased from 4 to 10 percent. Interestingly, Latinas are twice as likely to major in business than any other group.

During this same period, the high school dropout rate for Latinas decreased from 55 percent to 33 percent, but it still is three times higher than for white women. Teenage pregnancy among Latinas also remained high. Thus, even though Latinas have made tremendous social, economic and political strides, efforts to challenge and support young Latinas must continue.

Latina Entrepreneurship Research

Research on Hispanic entrepreneurship is very limited. Research on Latina business owners is even more scarce. However, a 1998 study published in *Small Business Management*[23] compared Hispanic men and women on 23 criteria and found interesting differences in personal background and business, organizational and financial characteristics.

Briefly, Latina business owners tended to be younger; therefore, they had less business experience and were less likely to be married than their male counterparts.

No differences were found in levels of education and degrees of acculturation. In fact, the education level of all respondents was relatively high. Fifty-one percent had bachelor's or graduate degrees and an additional 34 percent had some college-level education.

Differences were found in years in business, average number of employees and annual sales. Even though the range in number of years in business was wide, Latinas tended to own firms that were more recently established. Further, Latina firms had fewer employees and tended to generate smaller annual revenues than Latino-owned firms.

No differences were found for net profit margin, growth in sales and employment, type of business sector, legal status, path to business ownership, parental ownership of business or major target customers. The largest percentage of respondents was engaged in the service sector. More than half of all respondents indicated that their form of business organization was corporations, and the majority reported that they had started their own businesses instead of buying established businesses.

A comparison of perceived business problems showed only slight differences for Latinas. Sales and profit forecasting, ranked fifth by the entire group of respondents, was perceived to be slightly more difficult for female business owners. Obtaining lines of credit, ranked 11th by all respondents, also presented more difficulty for female owners. Further, Latinas perceived slightly greater difficulties in capital management, working capital management, pricing strategies, short-term business planning, labor cost analysis and debt management. Finally, Latinas reported a significantly higher level of gender problems – but this issue was ranked 59th out of 64. Other problems were perceived as more pressing. The authors of the study noted that most of these differences could be explained by the differences in years of experience.

International Trade

International trade is an important part of the U.S. and global economies. As of the third quarter of 1999, exports represented about 10.8 percent of the gross domestic product (GDP), and in the last decade have hovered between 9 percent and a little over 11 percent of the increasing GDP.[24] The importance of international trade will only increase as the trend toward globalization continues. But the importance of international trade goes beyond economics to global influence and leadership.[25] The value the United States puts on its role as a world leader can only increase.

Hispanic Business magazine summarized the essentials of U.S. trade for 1997 as follows:

The U.S. Department of Commerce breaks international trade into three categories: goods, services and income. By volume, the product category dominates with a United States export-import total of $155 trillion in 1997. However, just as in the domestic economy, the service sector shows dynamic growth. Since 1990, service exports from the United States have increased 75 percent to a 1997 total of $258.3 billion. During that same period, the income category – which includes royalties, licensing fees and yields from U.S.-owned assets abroad – has increased 48 percent to $241 billion. While the U.S. economy runs a deficit of $198 billion in goods and a slight deficit of $5 billion on income, the country enjoys a surplus of $87.7 billion in the service sector.[26]

Between 1987 and 1997, the number of small businesses that exported goods more than tripled, from 65,900 to 202,185,[27] accounting for 31 percent of total merchandise export sales. No comparable statistics are available for service sales, but with the large number of service firms among small businesses, the percentage of service export sales could easily equal or be higher than merchandise export sales.[28] In 1999, about 97 percent of firms that engaged in export trade were small businesses, according to the SBA.[29]

The rewards of international trade are many, according to the SBA's Office of International Trade (OIT):[30]

Small businesses that engage in international trade are stronger as companies and as contributors to their communities. Small business exporters bring stability and prosperity to their communities. Small businesses have a direct stake in their communities and typically remain in their communities, observing labor, environmental, and other state and federal regulations. Small business exporters tend to pay higher salaries. American workers producing for export earn 15 percent higher wages and receive 11 percent higher benefits than non-export workers. Companies engaged in export trade are 20 percent more productive and 9 percent more likely to stay financially solvent. They also experience 20 percent greater job growth than non-exporters.

Aida Alvarez, SBA administrator, makes the most convincing argument in favor of international trade: "With 96 percent of the world's population and 67 percent of the world's purchasing power located outside our borders, the potential for small business growth in international trade is huge."[31]

Yet the trade deficit continues its upward climb. In 1998, it was $164 billion, up substantially from each of the previous two years. By August 1999, the United States had surpassed the 1998 trade deficit.[32] This represents significant risk for entrepreneurs involved in international trade. Nevertheless, Isaac Cohen, director of the United Nations Economic Commission for Latin America and the Caribbean in Washington, D.C., projected in late 1997 that U.S. companies would continue to increase trade with Latin America at a national rate of about 10 percent per year.[33]

Adding to the risk involved, the ebb and flow of international commerce is affected by sociopolitical and economic factors in the United States and abroad. The strength of the U.S. dollar, internal policy regarding trade imbalances and global relations, international players and public opinion interact in a 24-hour business day for those entrepreneurs and businesses interested in the promising global market.

As the world market increasingly acts as an integrated whole, the effect nations' economies have on each other becomes more noticeable. When one economy has problems, others feel the effects – even if they are half a world away and seemingly unrelated. For instance, when the Asian monetary crisis arose in 1998, multinational companies in Latin America braced themselves, knowing a shortage of financing and investment capital would follow. They scaled back, canceled orders and rode the tide. That in turn affected U.S. Hispanic firms doing business in Latin America   Latin American orders were canceled or rescheduled, payment schedules were renegotiated and growth strategies reconsidered.

Hispanic Entrepreneurs and International Trade

International trade, with all its rewards and risks, is what many entrepreneurs dream of, and it appears that Hispanic entrepreneurs have the right stuff for this complex but lucrative area of business. As noted in Chapter 2, language and awareness of culture appear to be natural and unique competitive advantages for Hispanic entrepreneurs. According to *Hispanic Business*, Hispanic-owned businesses are active players in the continuous and steady rise of U.S. exports. The biggest Hispanic exporters are expanding more quickly than U.S. exporters overall.

Hispanic-owned businesses are the fastest growing among U.S. exporters. Growth has been recorded at 12.6 percent, according to the U.S Census.[34] Reports from the Office of International Trade (OIT) at the SBA support this: Minority-owned small businesses are more likely to export and to export more intensively than others. The SBA survey [35] also reveals that a greater proportion of Hispanic- and Asian-owned firms (2.7 percent and 2.3 percent, respectively) export than do white-owned firms (1.8 percent). These numbers reinforce the notion that there is a connection between ethnic minorities in the United States and their "ancestral or recent homelands that fosters international trade."

These limited statistics on Hispanic involvement in international trade suggest a strong presence. Additional evidence can be inferred from state trade information. States with large Hispanic populations and large numbers of Hispanic businesses – Florida, California and Texas – are leading in international trade.

Further, According to *Hispanic* magazine, U.S. exports to Latin America and the Caribbean accounted for 20 percent of all U.S. exports between 1990 and 1997.[36] Exports to just the Caribbean increased from $9 billion in 1989 to $221.1 billion in 1999.[37] According to the SBA's Office of International

Trade, U.S. exports to Latin America and the Caribbean increased 150 percent in the same period. These areas accounted for 40 percent of U.S. export growth between 1993 and 1997.[38] And, interestingly, the United States enjoys a trade surplus with most countries in Latin America and the Caribbean compared to the overall deficit worldwide.[39] This shows the growth potential for American businesses within these markets. Also, the tremendous growth of Hispanic-owned service companies, especially those supplying information technology and clean technology, may be leading the international service surge.

Factors Encouraging Trade with Latin America

Many factors contribute to the increased and continued presence of U.S. Hispanic entrepreneurs in international trade. These represent extraordinary opportunities for entrepreneurs interested in this market. These include increasing economic strength in Latin America and a growing market; availability of quality products in the U.S.; and an increase in privatization of state owed companies; and an increase in trade agreements among Latin American governments, and with European and Asian countries.

Increasing Economic Strength in Latin America

Latin American economies wavered in the last decade of the 20th century, but they show a trend toward recovery, stability and overall growth. This growth is spearheaded by Mexico, which, despite two monetary devaluations in the last decade – one as high as 70 percent – has emerged as the 10th largest economy in the world.[40] Mexico is the United States' second largest trading partner, second only to Canada and overtaking Japan.[41] According to *Hispanic Business*,[42] state-by-state totals on exports to Mexico show Texas leading the way with $21.8 billion, followed by California with $7.3 billion and Michigan with $3.1 billion. Arizona and Illinois export $2.1 billion and $1 billion in goods and services to Mexico, respectively.

A Growing Latin American Market

Increased political stability and economic growth have also fueled growth in the Latin American market. Latin America has been one of the fastest growing regions of the world, and the United States has been one of the main beneficiaries of this growth.[43] According to *Business Week*,[44] a new generation of Latin American companies run by managers with global expertise is growing rapidly in their home countries and throughout the region. These companies include both multinationals and companies focusing on the growing consumer class of Latin America. These new executives themselves form an interesting consumer market for U.S. Hispanic entrepreneurs.

Availability of High-Quality U.S. Products

The availability of high-quality products and efficient distribution networks in the United States is a tremendous opportunity for entrepreneurs. They can get high-demand products to the consumer in Latin America in record time, surpassing European and Asian competitors.

Partnerships with American firms have proven lucrative for corporate giants as well as entrepreneurial firms. As corporate America has taken notice of the Latin American market, it has positioned itself to take advantage of the geographic proximity of South Florida to Latin America and the growth of Hispanic entrepreneurial activity in

South Florida. According to *Hispanic Business* magazine,[45] most major high-tech businesses, especially computer manufacturers, have centralized operations in Florida. They include Epson, Canon, Apple, Toshiba, Hewlett-Packard, Microsoft and IBM. These firms in turn have attracted related industries: telecommunications, banking, and news media.

The result is a substantial amount of subcontracting and partnering with Hispanic entrepreneurs, among others, to tap into or develop distribution strategies in Latin America. An example is Hispanic firms working with major U.S. firms to sell computers in Latin America. When the personal computer market matured, the secondary market – printers, computer accessories and parts – presented a natural opportunity for entrepreneurs.

Microretailing, a Hispanic-owned firm featured in the *Hispanic Business* 500, illustrates this trend to connect suppliers to Latin American markets. Microretailing has an agreement with Hewlett-Packard to handle computer product sales in Central America and the Caribbean through a tight channel of distributors. The effort is coordinated from the Hewlett-Packard office in Miami.

Increasing Interest in Privatization

A 1997 *Hispanic Business* article entitled "Telecom Wars in Latin America"[46] discussed the trend toward privatization of businesses such as telephone companies. This makes investing in Latin America an attractive prospect to U.S. Hispanics and other entrepreneurs worldwide. The major telecommunications giants have established partnerships with local companies in each country in Latin America, beginning with Mexico. At stake is a $4 billion market in Mexico, which is expected to grow to $11 billion in the next five years after Mexico privatized its telephone company in January 1997. Other Latin American nations are following Mexico's lead.

Increasing Free Trade Agreements and World Interest

The 1999 annual meeting of the World Trade Organization (WTO) was evidence of the complexity of modern trade agreements. Important issues of sovereignty, labor and the environment, long connected with trade agreements but often ignored, are being reemphasized by a wide variety of organizations. Nevertheless, interest in securing commercial trade agreements continues to run high in Central and Latin America and the Caribbean.

Most Latin American economies are expected to grow at an annual rate of 4 to 8 percent for the next few years. "This growth has a driving force behind it – the free market of the Americas," according to Ramon Arias, CEO of Inter-American Management Consultants in Miami.[47]

This presents opportunities as well as risks for U.S. Hispanic entrepreneurs. After the North American Free Trade Agreement (NAFTA) was signed into law in 1993, bringing together Canada, Mexico and the United States as trade partners, it was expected that Chile would soon be a part of the agreement. This proposal stalled in Congress, as did fast-track authorization, but these events did not dampen efforts to increase trade agreements in Latin America.

Since then, approximately 15 trade agreements have been completed or are moving toward completion,[48] most without U.S. involvement, thus decreasing its leadership position within the region in matters of trade.[49] The intricacies of these agreements make passage a slow and lengthy process. Despite the inherent difficulties, the completion and use of such agreements are a testimony to their importance as acknowledged by countries in the western hemisphere and throughout the world.

The largest agreement is the Free Trade Area of the Americas (FTAA), which involves 34 countries. Meanwhile, MERCOSUR, a trade bloc led by Brazil and originally composed of Argentina, Uruguay, and Paraguay, has grown significantly. Since NAFTA went into effect, MERCOSUR has added Chile and Bolivia as associate members. And talks have opened with Peru, Ecuador, Colombia and Venezuela. Between 1990 and 1995, intra-MERCOSUR trade increased by 26 percent a year, and the MERCOSUR countries are setting the pace for the Free Trade Area of the Americas.

Other agreements include the Andean Pack, the Central American Common Market, the G3 and the Paraguay Round Agreement, to name a few. The region's imports increased by 127 percent and its exports by 73 percent between 1990 and 1996. During that period, intra-regional trade of all Latin American exports grew 18 percent.

Most significant are the international agreements that include Europe, Asia and Latin America. The European Community and Latin America have longstanding relationships – especially in Argentina, Brazil and Chile. More recently, the Asian link was strengthened in Peru following the election of President Alberto Fujimori, who is of Asian ancestry. European and Asian presences in Latin America are expected to increase as the number of trade agreements suggests.

Canada, Mexico and Chile have entered an agreement that gives their exports to each other an 11 percent lower tariff than those applied to U.S. exports. Interestingly, MERCOSUR has also established trade relations with Europe, as has Mexico through NAFTA-like agreements whose purpose is to increase foreign investment and decrease dependency on the United States.[50] Asian and European companies interested in the U.S. market have set up manufacturing companies[51] in Mexico to take advantage of the tariff breaks that Mexico enjoys through NAFTA.[52]

Finally, a longstanding idea to bring Central and South American and Caribbean countries under one coordinated currency has sparked renewed interest. The most recent proposal was to base a Latin American currency on a basket that includes the yen, the dollar and the euro.[53]

Summary

Hispanic entrepreneurs who participate in international trade have come full circle, heading back from the Americas to Europe and Asia, where their early ancestors originated. While the role of Hispanic entrepreneurs in U.S. economic prosperity and leadership is increasing, it does not seem to have one single milestone to mark its place. But the trends are strong and show tremendous progress. Hispanic-owned firms are increasing in record numbers. This is also true of their receipts, employment and payrolls.

Despite differences among the Hispanic-American subgroups, especially comparing the percentage of companies with the revenues they take in, the upward trend in all cases is remarkable. Hispanic-owned firms are represented in all industries but, following national trends, show a dramatic increase in business services. Most businesses are in states that have large populations of Hispanics – California, Texas and Florida. Again, following national norms, most Hispanic firms are sole proprietorships, followed by subchapter "S" corporations and partnerships. By percentage, sole proprietorships have decreased whereas subchapter "S" corporations have increased dramatically. Business receipts have also shown a substantial increase. Partnerships have shown a small but significant increase in percentage of firms and receipts.

This trend of increasing prosperity in Hispanic businesses is led by Latinas, who have elected to give themselves a promotion to president instead of waiting for corporations and government employers to give them their due. Latina leadership is evident in all areas – in government, corporate, and civic organizations.

Hispanics excelling in the complex area of international trade are reaching beyond Latin America and the Caribbean to Europe and Asia and this closes the circle.

Hispanic businesses have played a significant role in the gains made by Hispanics, particularly in the creation of wealth. The opportunity and the promise for continued prosperity must include the economic piece to complement the social and political gains made so far. Together these are a powerful force.

Notes

[1]Nicolás Kanello, *Hispanic Firsts: 500 Years of Extraordinary Achievements* (Houston, Texas: Arte Público Press, 1997).

[2]Charles Gonzalez, J. Reichert, and P. Caldwell, *Yes you Can! Every Latino's Guide to Building Family Wealth* (Worchester, Massachusetts: Chandler House Press, 1998).

[3]Beverly Vasquez, "Hispanics leading in business growth," *Denver Business Journal* (1996) September 13, 1A.

[4]Aida Alvarez, "Hispanic-owned business and the SBA," Small Business Administration: Outreach Initiatives – Hispanic fact sheet (1997).

[5]Jeff D. Vitucci and J. Russell, "The era of the entrepreneur," (Hispanicbusiness.com//research/20 anniv entrepreneur 0499.asp HispanTelligence, 1999).

[6]*Hispanic Business*, "The state of the Hispanic economy," *Hispanic Business* (1999) April, 22.

[7]Andrea Seidsma, "A summit of Entrepreneurs," *Hispanic Business* (1999) November, 20.

[8]*Hispanic Business*, "The state of the Hispanic economy."

[9]Small Business Administration (SBA), "Hispanic-Owned Businesses and the SBA: Outreach Initiatives-Hispanic Fact Sheet," (1999).

[10]U.S. Department of Commerce, Economics and Statistics Administration, *Hispanic-owned businesses: Reaching new heights* (Bureau of the Census, Statistical Brief. SB/96-4, 1996) August.

[11]Rick Mendosa, "Half a million jobs," *Hispanic Business* (1996) September, 16-18.

[12]Isaac Cohen, "1997:The business & economic agenda—The year ahead," *Hispanic Business* (1997) January, 10-12.

[13]Small Business Administration (SBA), *New report on growth of minority owned businesses* (Office of Advocacy, U.S. Number 99-16 ADVO, 1999) April 15.

[14]Edward Lowe Foundation, *1987 Census statistics Hispanic-owned small businesses* (1998) Document 1271.

[15]The National Foundation for Women Business Owners (NFWBO), "Minority women-owned firms thriving," NFWBO News (1997) 3rd Quarter.

[16]Anne Chen, "Latinas lead the nation in business entrepreneurship," *Knight-Ridder/Tribune News Service* (1999) February 11, K0986.

[17]Lee Romney, "Latinas get down to business," *Los Angeles Times Business and Technology Update* (Latimes.com, 1998) November.

[18]Chen.

[19]*Catalyst, Women of color in corporate management: A statistical picture,* U.S. Census data for 1994-1995. (www.catalystwomen.org, 1997) October 2.

[20]*Catalyst.*

[21]AFL-CIO, "It's time for working women to earn equal pay," *AFL-CIO Ask a working woman survey* (www.aflcio.org/home.htm, 2000).

[22]Romney.

[23]Soyeon Shim and M. Eastlick, *Journal of Small Business Management* (1998) July, 18.

[24]Council of Economic Advisers, *Economic Indicators* (Prepared for the Joint Economic Committee by the Council of Economic Advisers, United States Government Printing Office, 1999), December.

[25]Timothy White, "American participation in NAFTA," *International Journal on World Peace* (1998) December, 43(1).

[26]Joel Russell, "The import trade," *Hispanic Business* (1998) November, 28.

[27]U.S. Department of Commerce, Office of Trade and Economic Analysis, Trade Development/International Trade Agency, *Exporter Data Base and SME Exporter Profiles* (www.ita.doc.gov/industry/ot.smeseminar.pdf).

[28]Jan Beiting, "Beyond our borders: It's a big world of opportunities for minority and women exporters," *Minority Business Entrepreneur* (1998) July/August, 29-36.

[29]Small Business Administration (SBA): Office of International Trade (OIT), *America's small businesses and international trade: A report* (Office of International Trade and the Office of Communication and Marketing, 1999) November.

[30]SBA: Office of International Trade (OIT), *America's small businesses and international trade.*

[31]SBA: Office of International Trade (OIT), *America's small businesses and international trade.*

[32]SBA: Office of International Trade (OIT), *America's small businesses and international trade.*

[33]Maria Zate, "Getting ahead in the big city," *Hispanic Business,* (1997) October, 44-46.

[34]Joel Russell, "Beyond Latin America," *Hispanic Business* (1996) November, 34-43.

[35]Beiting.

[36]Kimberly Garcia, "Office sweet office," *Hispanic* (1999) January/February, 24-30.

[37]Francisco Flores, "The case for Caribbean trade enhancement: United States ready to approve free trade with area," *Journal of Commerce and Commercial Trade* (1999) October 19, 7.

[38]Kimberly Garcia, "Business Opportunities in Latin America," *Hispanic* (1999) January/February, 94.

[39]Joel Russell, "Chile's slow road to Fast Track," *Hispanic Business* (1997) November, 44.

[40]Carol Zabin, "U.S.- Mexico Relations: Labor Market Interdependence" (book review), *Industrial and Labor Relations Review* (1994) January, 336-338.

[41]Antonio J. Villamil, "Latin American trade set for growth in 1998," *Hispanic Business* (1998) January/February, 22.

[42]Russell, "Chile's slow road to Fast Track."

[43]Antonio O. Garza Jr., "NAFTA Window of opportunity is not completely closed," *Hispanic Business* (1997) May, 34-44.

[44]Geri Smith, E. Malkin, I. Katz, A. Mandel-Campbell and J. Pearson, "The new Latin corporation," *Business Week* (1997) October 27, 71-82.

[45]Joel Russell, "How does Miami do it?" *Hispanic Business* (1997) November, 34-46.

[46]Cary Cardwell, "The telecom wars," *Hispanic Business* (1997) May, 44-46.

[47]Russell, "Chile's slow road to Fast Track."

[48]Robert Devlin and R. French Davis, "Towards an evaluation of regional integration in Latin America in the 1990s," *World Economy* (1999) March, 261-264.

[49]Murray L. Weidenbaum, "Is America Slipping in International Trade?" *USA Today* (magazine) (1999) July, 20.

[50]Howard LaFranchi, "Today, NAFTA, mañana, Europe! say Mexico traders: President Zedillo and EU push pact for freer trade and less dependency on the U.S.," *The Christian Science Monitor* (1999) April, 6-7.

[51]Debra O'Hara, "Not much - yet: Compared with Arizona, California and Texas, New Mexico's trade with Mexico is minuscule, but a change in the wind," *New Mexico Business Journal* (1999) September/October, 55.

[52]Joel Millman, "Asian firms plunge into Mexico on NAFTA's promise: Investment is boon to manufacturing," *The Wall Street Journal* (1998) August 14, A13(W)-A13(E).

[53]*The Economist*, "MERCOSUR: Becalmed," *The Economist* (US) (1999) December 11, 34.

PART II

HISPANIC
ENTREPRENEURS
AND THEIR
STORIES

Introduction to the Biographies

The following biographraphical accounts are the reflections of highly successful Hispanic entrepreneurs. As such, they are contemplative, sometimes intimate and, above all, inspirational. They show that there are many roads to success; to travel them requires deep commitment and hard work. But the results are both satisfying and fulfilling. Finally, they show that an individual's success is the success of a whole community.

The biographies were collaborative efforts, involving interviews with 30 of the top Hispanic entrepreneurs in the United States. All of their stories were compelling and uplifting. The six included in this book were selected to reflect the diversity of cultural subgroups and national origin, industries of specialization, gender and geography.

The entrepreneurs were interviewed and tape recorded, and transcripts were then summarized to reflect each person's values and special interests. Their accounts were written as first-person narratives to capture each person's unique view and convey – through his or her own words, style and tone – the nature of the entrepreneurial experience. Finally, participants were asked to review a draft for content and accuracy and to ensure it reflected their personal communication style.

The entrepreneurial experience, especially the high growth experience, is about change. We can expect that the companies featured here will not stay static, but will evolve, resize, grow and continue to change. It is an exciting journey for which these entrepreneurs are well prepared. We look forward to learning from the experiences they are helping to create.

We would like to thank all the entrepreneurs who shared their stories and hopes, so that these and others to be told in future books will provide valuable seeds for thought and action.

CHAPTER FOUR

Danny Villanueva
We Were Pioneers

BASTION CAPITAL CORPORATION
LOS ANGELES

Industry: Venture Capital and Investments

Date started: November 12, 1992

Size of Fund: $125 million

Percentage of Growth in 1999: 30%

Awards, Board Memberships and Accomplishments

One of the founders of Univisión, Inc.

Major investor in Telemundo Group, Inc.

2000 Commissioner – National Commission
on Entrepreneurship

1998 Founder of Destino 2000 – The Hispanic
Legacy Fund, The Ventura County Foundation

Soon after the proposed sale of Telemundo Group, Inc. – the second largest Spanish-language television company in the United States – to Sony was announced, my partners and I suggested that Sony begin meeting industry people and organizations. The Association of Hispanic Advertising Agencies meeting in Miami was a perfect place for Sony executives to lay out their vision for Spanish broadcasting. They were prepared to explore new concepts in programming and marketing, using their vast resources and those of partner TCI.

The agency people sensed that, at last, they would have the choices that are part of a competitive environment. John Feltheimer of Sony took advantage of the opportunity. Sony meant change as well as choice. Spanish-language broadcasting had been part of my life for over a quarter century. For me, this was a new day.

It also was special for me because I got to visit old friends in our business. One speaker said, referring to me, "We have a special friend with us. He is a partner in Telemundo and a pioneer in our business." Later that day, I heard someone say that many would not be there had it not been for a crazy bunch of guys who had plowed ahead with their vision, when it might have been more prudent to fold up the tent and give up the fight.

My mind wandered in and out of the incredible 30-year odyssey as I visited with friends and colleagues. We had put everything on the line – personal guarantees and all – to maintain the battle. When making each payroll was a drama and trauma, we believed we had a mission that went way beyond business; that sense of commitment and obligation kept us going.

We were the first UHF (ultra high frequency) broadcasters when television sets could not receive our signal without a special converter that had to be purchased separately. We were also the first broadcasters who went on the air with no viewers. Our first ratings claim was a letter from the converter manufacturer confirming that they had sold 2,000 units in the Los Angeles area …

My thoughts went back to Don Emilio Azcárraga Vidaurreta, the founder of the largest producer of Spanish-language programming in the world – Mexico's Grupo Televisa S.A. Don Emilio was known for his vision, generosity and compassion. I remembered our first meeting in a Los Angeles restaurant. I did not know it was an audition, yet I was nervous meeting a man who seemed to transcend the normal standards of greatness.

Afterward, René Anselmo – Mr. Azcárraga's representative in the United States – smiled and patted me on the back, saying simply, "Don Emilio likes you." It was my introduction to a great family that founded the Mexican television industry and later brought Spanish-language broadcasting to the United States. It was a defining moment in my life.

It was also the first time that I spent any significant time with René – Reynold Anselmo – who was from Boston of Italian descent. He was, however, more Latin than any of us. He had been involved in Broadway productions in Mexico, and then began working for Don Emilio selling TV shows. He quickly became a major player in Televisa and was treated like a member of the Azcárraga family. Don Emilio sent René to the United States to start the Spanish-language TV station that later became Univisión …

Years later, when the call came that Don Emilio had died, I raced to the airport to fly to Mexico City. I walked into the front room of his house and saw his coffin. Standing before it was his son, Emilito, who was now the keeper of the vision. Emilito said "¿Qué hubo, Danny (What's up, Danny)?" I could not think of anything to say except, "God bless you, Emilio," as I hugged him.

Don Emilio's longtime assistant, Amalia, said that because I was the youngest, I should stay with the coffin through the night. It was strange *haciendo guardia* (standing guard) by a coffin. This was not part of my custom. I was not comfortable. Around 2 or 3 a.m., I heard a commotion outside. Through the door came the president of Mexico, Luis Echevarría.

He was red-eyed, intense. He stood by the coffin a few minutes, head bowed, then stormed out the door with his entourage. Some of my friends were not surprised at this episode, because Echevarría was known to work ungodly long hours. I have to admit, he looked scary to me ...

As my mind raced on, I saw the international telethon we organized to help the victims of the 1985 Mexico City earthquake. With few resources and just 10 days to prepare, we brought together Julio Iglesias, Placido Domingo, Sammy Davis Jr. and many other stars. In seven hours we raised close to $15 million for the American Red Cross. It was one of our finest efforts as a fledgling network built on idealism and compassion for our brothers and sisters.

In the rush to get the show on the air, we forgot that Herb Albert was sitting in the guest trailer waiting to be called. But, he was so gracious. He didn't complain. He went on stage, performed and gave us a check for $25,000 ...

I will never forget Ricardo Montalban, who also responded to a call to duty. He was with us at Rubén Salazar's funeral. And he was also with us when we launched our Christmas telethon, now in its 27th year. I know history will be very kind to this man, who was a giant on and off screen ...

Again, René entered my thoughts, sitting in a lawn chair by his Winnebago in front of the World Trade Center in New York. He had started a hunger strike because the Port Authority, which owned the World Trade Center, had reneged on a promise to put our antenna on the building. I am convinced he would have died if the Port Authority leaders had not finally kept their word. That hunger strike affected his health, but that was René ...

I remembered the coroner's office in Los Angeles, where I identified Rubén Salazar's body. He had been shot by a sheriff's deputy at the height of a demonstration protesting the high number of young Latinos dying in Vietnam ...

I remembered the biggest bank in California telling me that our station's loan was the worst in the loan officer's portfolio and that we would have to go elsewhere. I saw "Spic station" scrawled across the door of our studio, the bomb that damaged the neighboring gas station and the armed guard we had on our roof to protect our employees. I remembered the threats, the taunts and our concerns for our families during that turbulent period ...

Through all of that, we had persevered – Emilito, René, Emilio Nicolás (Nicky), Julian (Julie) Kaufman, Frank Fouce and the rest of that crazy bunch of guys who had invested their lives to the vision of Spanish-language television in the United States.

Oh, yes, we picked up a Peabody Award for Public Service, but the price was damnable. René and Emilito are gone. Of all the partners, Nicky and I are the only two still alive, but we have not spoken in years. Perhaps the pain is too much for us ...

A lifetime passed in that flashback.

We were builders. We followed the dream, and time had taken its toll, but now we were vindicated. Sony and Wall Street were signatories to that fact, as Univisión and Telemundo entered a new era. Spanish-language broadcasting had taken wing and was soaring.

If I had to do it all over, I would choose again to be a builder, even with all the heartaches. It was the opportunity of a lifetime, a chance to make a difference in people's lives, and we made the most of it. We were pioneers, all right. God knows we lived with passion and a sense of mission. As I used to tell my mom, "That station is my pulpit, Mom, and I'm preaching!"

Mi Familia – My Family

My father and mother, Primitivo Villanueva Villegas and Pilar Ramos de Villanueva, met and married in Guanajuato, Mexico, when they were both 15. They had two children who were stillborn and two who died shortly before the family moved to the United States – a tremendous blow to my parents. Of the remaining 12, I am number nine.

I was born in Tucumcari, New Mexico where my family settled. We later moved to Phoenix and then to Calexico, California. That's where I grew up, and I consider it my home.

"¡Cabezón!" (Hard Headed)

My mother was tough – her discipline, determination and power held us together all those years. We owe much to that illiterate but wise woman who transformed herself, as she used to say, from an *indita* (a little Indian woman) into a formidable force in our lives.

Mom worked as a domestic and as a tortilla maker in a local factory. She and women from nearby border towns worked 10 hours a day, sitting around a huge hotplate making tortillas and talking. Those tortilla makers, my sisters told me, were instrumental in changing my mother's ideas about life and family. She took charge of the family and never relinquished it, and she single-handedly changed my father, who had been struggling with the loss of those two babies early in their marriage.

Mom always loved music. On her way home from work, she used to stop at a little storefront church to listen to the singing. It was her way to forget the hotplate and hard life. At first, she sat in the back and listened. Pretty soon, she joined in the singing and listened to the talking. Before long, she was part of the church. Then she dragged my dad in, and he became part of the group. He later became a preacher.

My brothers and sisters say my mother had me pegged. I cannot remember a time when I wasn't her project. Even years later, when I was playing in the NFL, she asked me to call her every week. I don't know if she asked my other brothers and sisters to do the same, but I dutifully called every week, like clockwork, from wherever I was in the world – Brazil, Mexico, other places in Latin America. I kept my promise to her until she passed away in 1980 at the age of 80.

After all these years, I can still hear her calling me *cabezón* (hard headed) ...

She worried about me. She complained about me. She called me *cabezón* because I was stubborn. Everyone laughed when she did that. She lectured me every chance she got, and I guess there were plenty of opportunities.

In my favorite photograph of Mom, she is pointing her finger in front of my nose. I can remember that day so clearly. She thought I was getting too much publicity during the Watts riots. She believed we should all be anonymous in the mass of people. She worried that I stood out. It was a violent time, and she was probably right to be worried.

Her *regañadas* (scoldings) were usually on target. She had incredible intuition and said things that amazed and stunned me with their depth. Yet, she put them in such simple terms, because that was the only way she knew. She taught through *dichos* (sayings, proverbs and aphorisms). She never failed to have at least one saying for any situation, and then she would throw in a biblical story to top it off.

My Mother on Money

My mother told me, *"Si lo haces por dinero, vas a fracasar."* (If money is the reason for doing anything, if that is your driver ... you are doomed to fail). "Money" was the start of a sermon on the biblical story of the money changer in the temple. "Don't ever be a money changer," she said. "Do not ever worship money; because if you do, you will fail. Do the right thing and work hard at it."

My Mother on Philanthropy

"*Él que no da no recibe.*" (You have to give to receive). Give. Give. Give. Most of her *regañadas* had to do with giving or being of service to others. She would say, "*Hijito* (son), God blesses all of us with different degrees of talent. Some of us are more talented than others, but we all have the capacity to be *agradecidos* (grateful). No matter how bad off you are, be grateful that you are better off than others." She never let me think that I was bad off, that I was tired, that my life was hard or that we were poor. She said, "You are blessed because you have the ability to help other people, to do something for someone else."

To this day, I remember every inflection of her voice. "Success should not be measured by how much you have but by how much you give back." She believed philanthropy was a natural antidote to the worship of money. She said, "Give it away. It will come back to you many times."

My Mother on Getting Ahead and Taking Risks

"*Camarón que se duerme se lo lleva la corriente* (a sleeping shrimp is swept away by the current). Don't fall asleep; stay alert. Be prepared to take advantage of opportunities when they arise."

Preparation meant getting an education and working hard. Mom was convinced there were windows of opportunity in life as well as business. "When those windows open, you must first recognize them and then know what to do ...

be prepared to step through them." Sometimes those opportunities last only seconds. Then you have to *meterle ganas* (go all out) to take advantage of them.

The formula for getting ahead was education, energy, courage, wisdom and instinct. With eyes opened wide and hands held up to her face for emphasis, Mom would say, *"Ten los ojos abiertos* (keep your eyes open)."

Preparation is a basic and essential part of taking risks. Beyond preparation, she would say, "Take chances, hope for luck and trust your instincts. *Siempre con fé* (have faith). Have faith in God, faith in yourself and faith in your ideas."

My Mother on Leadership

My mother believed that leadership was a two-edged sword. While leaders were important, she also felt there was something wrong with standing out, with being outstanding. She worried when she read articles about me. I was both newscaster and operations manager at KMEX during the East Los Angeles riots. Her worries were well-founded, especially when Rubén, our news director, was killed in 1970.

"No te pongas crema en los tacos (don't lose your perspective). Always remember where you came from, *mijito* (my son)." It was good advice; it keeps me grounded. She insisted, "Keep going back to where you came from."

I go back home when I sense the need to recharge. For instance, in anticipation of the Telemundo and Sony deal, I went to Calexico. I drove around and visited old friends and old places. Calexico, down on the border where Mom and Dad are buried, is where I go for strength and reassurance. It is my spiritual home.

Mom did much more than lecture. I can remember a time as a child, when polio was a big fear. My legs would give out while I was walking or running, and no one knew why. Ruth Ferguson, the missionary at the neighborhood house, took me to a doctor in San Diego. The doctor determined that my problem revolved around malnutrition. In a big family, if you miss a meal you get left out. I often ate things that were not good for me. With guidance, my mother changed my diet as much as she could.

More importantly, the doctor put me on a regimen of running. Three days a week, my mother woke me up early in the morning saying, *"Levántate mijito, es tiempo para correr* (wake up, my son, it is time to run). *Vamos a correr."* This went on all summer. Her persistence and encouragement made a fundamental difference in my life. The weakest part of my body became my strongest asset.

Athletics, Public Service and Entrepreneurship

As a student at Calexico High School, I took a good look at myself in the mirror. I was short, fat and slow. I would never be able to compete in basketball. My competitive advantages were my legs. I could learn to kick a football instead. I realized that if I worked really hard, I could be a pretty good kicker. I was determined that no one would ever outwork me. I made myself into a kicker because that was my ticket. I simply willed it.

People told me, "You are just a good little high school player, but you are not good enough to play at the college level." Did they have to say *little*? In response, I worked and worked and worked. I played football at New Mexico State University, where I majored in English, Spanish and journalism and ran the campus newspaper. I did not see professional football as an option in my future, so I decided to be an English teacher.

During my senior year I made an exceptionally long kick against the University of New Mexico. Chuck Benedict, a scout for the Rams, was in the stands. Later I was told that he wrote my name among his notes. Before spring training, the Rams knew they needed a kicker. Chuck looked up my name in his notebook and called the university. They gave him the number at the high school in Las Cruces, New Mexico, where I was doing my student teaching.

I got a note from the school office saying I had a call from Bob Waterfield of the Rams, and I made some sort of wise-crack. The office staff said, "This is for real, Danny. You have a call waiting." Despite all my hard work in college, the NFL had never been interested in me. Now I had an offer to try out with the Rams.

I found myself with a chance and a choice. I could try out as a free agent with the Rams, making $5,400 for the season, or I could teach English. I wondered if I could compete. Yet I knew I had to try or I would wonder for the rest of my life. So I told my family, my wife, Myna, and my little son, Danny Jr., "I need you to go along with me. I need to do this." Myna had left school and taken a job so I could study. With her backing, I went to Los Angeles to pursue a dream.

I survived training camp and made the team. I soon found out I *could* compete with my idols, the players I had watched play and read about. I worked even harder. I was in the NFL from 1960 to 1968. One season I scored 113 points, and twice I came close to wearing a Super Bowl ring when we played the Green Bay Packers.

I was the only Latino playing in the NFL, and I felt a responsibility to give back to our community. I started a campaign visiting schools, doing guest appearances – at PTAs, boys' and girls' clubs and YMCAs. I encouraged kids to stay in school and their parents to get involved in their children's education.

I visited the schools on my own time, as often as my budget would allow. Because my starting salary in the NFL was small and I had a wife and son to support, my program began on a very small scale. Later, with help from the Ford Dealers of Southern California, it grew.

I remember a conversation I with Jerry Simmons at Metromedia, now Fox Broadcasting, who asked how my school campaign was going. I said, "It is hard, but important." Without my knowing it, he talked to the Ford dealers in Southern California about this program and they agreed to help. They gave me a $500-a-month stipend for gas and a new Ford to drive. They also named the program the Ford Youth Program. I did 130 appearances a year under Ford's sponsorship.

My biggest blessing was an unexpected opportunity. One day while I was practicing, working hard to keep my position on the team, Simmons came to see me again. "Danny, my son is not really gifted athletically. He is a good learner and he works hard. Can you teach him to be a kicker?" I agreed. Little did I know, this window of opportunity would be one of my life's milestones.

I used to come early to practice and Simmons' son would be waiting for me. We would work hard and then I would say, "OK, I have to go to practice now." Or I'd stay after practice to work with him. "OK, let's work for half an hour and then I have to run." I shoehorned him into my schedule to help him. I did it because his dad was such a nice man.

As it turned out, his dad was a big man at Metromedia Fox. One day he said, "Danny, I am going to introduce you to Bert Avedon, who runs KMEX, the local Spanish-language television station." He not only introduced me, he arranged for the Ford Dealers to sponsor my show on the station.

I did sports commentary, and KMEX loved it because Ford was paying them. Additionally, the Ford Dealers increased their support of my youth program, cementing a nine-year relationship with Ford, both on and off the air. Then Coca-Cola volunteered, "If Ford sponsors you on Mondays, Wednesdays and Fridays, we will sponsor you on Tuesdays and Thursdays." This started my career in television.

Children had a special place in my life; so, I was pleased when I realized they were listening even more intently than they had at the beginning of my athletic career. To them, I was not an adult. I was not a policeman and I was not a parent. I was an athlete, so I was OK.

My interest in community service through television grew as I realized I could teach, influence opinion, and affect events. As I look back, I can say I was interested in making a difference, not in making a fortune. I remember a conversation with my dad when I kidded him, saying, "My pulpit reached more people than yours." He was genuinely amused, and proud of my career.

By now, I was playing for the Dallas Cowboys. My life became more hectic – family, football, television and community service. Eventually, it took its toll on me, both physically and mentally. I would commute to Los Angeles from Dallas to record five shows, return to Dallas in time for practice and continue to work with kids in between. This had a lot to do with my decision to retire from football at 29 with two years to go on my contract.

The scale tilted in January 1968 at the "Ice Bowl" in Green Bay. It is now referred to as the greatest game in NFL history, and it was to be my last time on the field. The wind-chill factor was 42 degrees below zero. We were winning with time running out, and I could literally feel the ring on my finger. Then, in the last seconds of the game, Green Bay Coach Vince Lombardi called a quarterback sneak, and the Packers won by four points. I figured I was not meant to wear the ring. It was time to retire. It was time to move on with my life.

I walked into the locker room. Coach Tom Landry was sitting on the rubdown table. He looked sad, so I decided to talk to him later. But in my mind, I retired at that moment. Despite my resolution, I went to work out after a few weeks. I had trouble putting on my football shoes. That was the only sign I needed. I put my sneakers on and went home. I put my football shoes in the closet and told Myrna, "I am done. I am retired."

In 1967, my football contract with the Cowboys paid me $18,000 a year. I took a 50 percent cut to work at KMEX.

KMEX and Spanish-Language Television

When I made the decision to go into UHF television, I was told I was making a terrible mistake. Spanish, the wisdom went, was a dead-end language and Spanish television was a dead-end business. Soon, all of us (Latinos) would be speaking English. My instincts told me there was an opportunity here, but there was risk involved – I did not understand the business, and my Spanish was terrible. Still, my gut told me this was my destiny.

My decision to move into Spanish-language television was based on my desire for public service, although I did not realize it then. I just knew this was something I had to do. I know in retrospect what motivated me. I come from a family of public servants, starting with my father. He was a saintly man who would help anyone out and never ask anything in return.

Yes, it was a risky business. Spanish-language UHF television was in its infancy. I figured I would get inside, work hard, learn the business and find a way of making it successful. What I lacked in knowledge and intelligence, I made up for in hard work. I opened the doors in the morning and closed them at night. I worked long hours, six days a week for years. I made myself into a broadcaster because I had to.

I started at KMEX as sports director. Within about a month, I also became news director. A few months later I became operations director. Then I took on community service. I kept taking on more and more responsibility. And in turn became station manager, general manager, vice president and then president. Finally, I became a partner in the parent company. And then we sold the whole thing to Hallmark Cards, Inc.

My Spanish Was Terrible

Although I moved up quickly, my television career was not all easy-going, especially at first. My command of formal, commercial, spoken Spanish was weak. I was the first non-foreign-born person to work as a regular on Spanish-language television. The audience was intolerant of incorrect Spanish, and I was criticized severely and loudly.

Even though Spanish was my first language, neither the street Spanish I used with friends (Spanglish) nor the Spanish I spoke with my parents was what broadcasters used. Commercial Spanish is very fast and much more formal. It is forceful, and the diction is somewhat exaggerated.

Growing up, I came to believe that speaking Spanish was a disadvantage. I became an English teacher to overcome that perceived disadvantage. Still, I also majored in Spanish. I did not realize it fully then, but I must have had a sense that speaking Spanish was an advantage.

In my new job, I had to learn to speak commercial Spanish quickly. I read Spanish-language newspapers in front of a mirror at home. I spent hours in front of the mirror. To my amazement, people who had once criticized me now became my strongest allies. I got calls from parents who were using me as an example for their children. "Look at him," they said. "Remember how he was when he started? Listen to his Spanish now." I had won them over through hard work.

KMEX, Advocacy Journalism and the Chicano Movement — the L.A. Riots

The East Los Angeles disturbances and our goal of positioning KMEX as a community leader coincided. It did not take much to see the urgent need for education and services in our community. My message never changed from when I began doing public appearances as an athlete: Get involved!

Parents, get involved with your children and their education. Kids, get involved in your schools. Have respect for education. Have respect for adults.

The dropout rate appalled me and many others. It is still a national tragedy. The lack of involvement by parents also appalled me. Yet, I understood it. My own parents visited my school a total of three times – the three times I received degrees. I could see why they didn't visit more often. My mom could not read or write. Neither of my parents could speak English. School was foreign to everyone, children and parents alike. Consequently, kids were dropping out, compromising their futures and the future of our community.

Then, students walked out at Lincoln Heights High School in Los Angeles. My instincts told me this was a defining moment. In fact, it ignited the Chicano Movement.

We at KMEX went to Lincoln Heights High, filmed the walkout and rushed back to the station. I did not want to wait for evening news coverage of the walkout. So I opened the door to the control booth saying, "I want to break into the programming to cover this story. Latino students were claiming they were not getting an education and had walked out led by a teacher, Sal Castro." The station operator responded, "We are not going to do it and I don't think you have the authority to order it." I felt so strongly about this that I said, "You have two options. You can cut into the programming and I will take full responsibility, or you are going to have to whip my ass." He looked at me and said, "OK, this is on *your* ticket."

We did a newsbreak, covered it on the evening news and did a special show with guests interviewed from both sides of the issue.

Our general manager was in Mexico. When he returned, I was sure he was going to fire me. But instead, he promoted me. I became station manager. Soon after, he had a disagreement with the board of directors and left. I replaced him.

Advocacy Journalism

When I became news director at KMEX, I knew I had to make a critical decision about the direction of the news. As I saw it, we had two choices. We could practice orthodox journalism and report events as they happened, or we could take a very high-risk tack, which I later described as advocacy journalism.

Advocacy journalism is a journalism of involvement, and it is a two-edged sword. We knew that although we were doing good things, we could get the community and ourselves into a lot of trouble. In practical terms, we literally made decisions about coverage based on the answer to the question, "Is this good for our community? If it is, let's make it happen. If it is bad, let's stop it." We understood the risks we were taking.

We began to take on causes about which we felt strongly, tackling them both as advocates and as reporters. There were plenty of opportunities to get involved in worthwhile issues. The immediate advantage was that the community finally had its own voice. The disadvantage, which evolved, was that the community did not like the idea of balancing viewpoints.

This made our job very hard. We were embraced as the community's voice to the exclusion of the "other side." When we tried to air a balanced story, some community leaders got angry. They had a voice through KMEX that they had never had in the general media, and were not about to share it. This widened the gap between the community and the "other side."

I understood the Latino community; I had been there, and I knew what they were saying and feeling. Still, I struggled with my journalistic instincts for balanced reporting. Once, as I was finishing an interview on a labor strike story and getting ready to interview management, the person I had just interviewed asked, "Where are you going?"

I answered, "I am going to get the other side of the story. That is what we do in journalism." The response was quick and resolute: "No, they have their own TV. To hell with them. We gave you our side." I understood that view, but I struggled with it.

Law enforcement perceived us as biased. I remember when the police kicked Chapo, our cameraman, and me off the Roosevelt High School campus during the second in a string of school walkouts. Kids were herded onto football fields and put into buses. Then the police took them away. As I walked alongside the buses, holding the kids' hands and trying to calm them down, a policeman tapped me on the shoulder and told me to leave. He said I was not a reporter, and this was not part of my job.

We were proud and humbled to win the 1970 Peabody Award for public service, *Peace in Our Time: KMEX-TV and the Death of Rubén Salazar*. We shared the award with the CBS Reports program, *The Selling of the Pentagon*. We received the award for our role in the movement as advocacy journalists and my particular role during the Chicano Moratorium.

Those were very, very tough times, volatile times. Out of that turmoil and uncertainty, KMEX assumed a very unusual leadership role. We had a unique responsibility and felt morally bound to it.

Hard life lessons came from the role we selected for ourselves.

Rubén Is Killed

The walkout in East Los Angeles was one of two defining moments. The second was when Rubén Salazar, our news director, was killed on August 29, 1970. I will never be able to describe the feelings that drowned my body as the coroner unveiled what was left of Rubén.

He had been working at KMEX for more than a year and had replaced me as news director. He had earned everyone's respect and friendship. In those days, the whole station was family. We supported each other to keep from falling apart emotionally. The last time I saw him alive was during a briefing, when we discussed what he was going to do before he left that evening.

As I was leaving, I said, "See you on Monday," and Rubén responded, "Yeah, if I make it out." He had acted strangely all day. He cleaned his office, which he never did, and insisted on knowing if the park where the march was to convene was in the city or the county. It turns out the park, now Salazar Park, is one block outside the city; but we never figured out why this was important to him.

Rubén had taken a break at the Silver Dollar Cafe, two blocks from the park where the march was to convene. Out of nowhere, a disturbance broke out just outside the Silver Dollar. Rubén stood up and yelled at our cameraman and reporter, "Get down." At that moment, a tear gas canister, fired through a little curtain that kept the bar dark, went through Rubén's head.

We will never know whether it was a freak accident or a homicide. Some people were hoping it would go to trial. The case closed with a settlement of $800,000, and we never knew what happened or why. I later saw official documents. Two-thirds of the text was blacked out for security reasons. This, of course, added to the mystery.

Rubén's death was significant to our community for many reasons. The loss was devastating to his family as well as the station family, but it strengthened our resolve to continue our leadership and responsibility to the community.

The Movement and My Turning Point

Between the walkout and Rubén's death, the movement became broader but still had no defined scope. It was taking new form as a shockingly large number of brown-skinned bodies began returning from the war in Southeast Asia. In addition to unequal education, the focus included the unequal rate at which Hispanic soldiers were dying.

For me, the turning point came as I was covering one of many marches and got swept along by the crowd. I remember clearly the sounds of bullets ricocheting beyond me. I saw outsiders – non-Hispanics – inciting our young people to violence. They were handing out liquor, beer and pamphlets. Again, our kids were being used as cannon fodder.

We never really knew who those inciters were. Ultimately, it did not matter. The incident left me with the recognition of how easily "they" could take advantage of us. Our emotions and passions made us easy pickings.

Nuestro Canal 34 – The Business

Essentially, our journalism had become entwined with the movement. It forever put KMEX in a unique position in the media. People saw us differently than any other media. The community referred to us as *"Nuestro Canal 34 (our* channel 34)."* Our audience felt they were our partners. We were in this together. It was an amazing, unique relationship and an unforgettable experience.

But my unique position had its disadvantages. It meant being away from my family. It meant working long hours and some risk. But we did some good work. We successfully exposed a judge who had ordered the sterilization of a Latina because she had given birth to a child while on welfare. We drew attention to politicians who were trying to shut down the Melabar Education Project, a bilingual test program. We also got involved in such everyday things as trash pickup and programs for the elderly.

As a business, KMEX took off like a rocket. The station went from struggling to make payroll in 1966 to grossing about $90,000 the year I took over. When I left in 1989 we had made $17 million. We had 30 employees when I took over, and we turned the station over with 150 employees. It was a success story, but it did not happen overnight. It took time and – literally – blood, sweat and tears. It was a monument to commitment and perseverance.

Growth

Once the riots subsided and KMEX established itself as a business, we were ready for growth. So we began a series of acquisitions and turnarounds.

We identified Channel 23 in Miami as a potential first purchase. The station was bankrupt, but we had done our homework and saw tremendous potential. Fidel Castro came to power in Cuba in 1959, and the first wave of Cuban immigrants was solidly working their way into the Miami economic structure when we purchased Channel 23 in 1971. The former owner lived in Los Angeles and did not appreciate what was happening in Miami. We switched to a Spanish-language format and later sold the station for around $50 million dollars.

I was earning about $15,000 a year when we purchased Channel 23. When my boss approached me about joining the venture, I did not dare mention I had no money to put on the deal. I had an opportunity to buy 10 percent of the station for $33,000 – twice my annual salary. I had faith but no money. The seller's financial representative said, "You are not strong enough financially, Danny. We are going to need a guarantee from you." He was right.

I managed to scrape up the guarantee from a good friend. My friend's wife, however, was not too happy with the transaction or me. Fortunately, I was never asked for the document. I was able to return the guarantee to my friend. He was off the hook with his wife, and so was I.

We quickly merged our stations in New York, Los Angeles and San Antonio with Miami, forming what became known as Spanish International Communication Corporation, Inc. or SICC, the forerunner of Univisión.[1] We had big plans for this station and for our company. The SICC partnership included Don Emilio Azcárraga Vidaurreta[2] owner of Televisa, S.A., in Mexico, and René Anselmo, each with 20 percent of the company. Don Emilio was not permitted to own more than that, according to Federal Communications Commission (FCC) regulations. The rest of us – Nicky, Julie, Frank Fouce, a couple of other investors and I – owned minority shares.

Televisa is the largest producer of Spanish-language programming in the Americas. Don Emilio had suggested we start a Spanish-language TV network in the United States. He formed a sister company – the Spanish International Network, or SIN – in 1961 as an export subsidiary. He deferred payment for programming, a generous act that would later haunt us.

Through SIN, Televisa planned to expand into the young but promising U.S. Latino market. René Anselmo presided over both SICC and SIN. By 1983, they were reaching 3.3 million Hispanic households.

Univisión Is Born

In 1976, Emilio, René and I sat in Emilio's office in Mexico City planning something dramatic and different. Emilio and René had decided that Televisa would do a Mexican salute to the United States for its bicentennial celebration. We would transmit live from Mexico City on the Raúl Velasco show "Siempre en Domingo (Always on Sunday)," using land-based lines. It would be a first, because we rarely did live television in those days. Our programming consisted of taped Televisa shows that we rotated among all our U.S. stations.

The live program *"Un Saludo de México en Su Aniversario* (A Greeting from Mexico on Your Anniversary)" was a smashing success. Viewers had never seen a show live from Mexico before, and they became very emotional. People called in crying, because it made them feel so close to Mexico. It was an incredibly emotional, if not financial, success.

Emilio knew live programming was special. He said, "Lets expand it and run live programming on the weekends." So we did: boxing every Saturday night, soccer games on Sunday afternoons and *"Siempre en Domingo"* on Sunday nights. Then we added a variety show to the lineup.

We needed a name for our new offering. The name *Univisión* came to me early in the discussion. To me, it meant television that united two countries. Other names were suggested, and my idea did not get much attention at first. Emilio wrote each of them on his ever-present chalkboard. Eventually we returned to *Univisión*, and we launched the weekend live programming under that banner. This eventually became the name of the public corporation.

On the Mountain

Our company grew and became financially stable, so we sought ways to expand. In 1980, René decided to look into a new technology, Low Power Television (LPTV) – transistors interconnected by satellite. With a 15-mile power radius, it enabled us to get into smaller markets without the overhead of stand-alone television stations.

When we decided to build our seventh and final station[3] in Phoenix, we faced our toughest obstacles. Neighbors opposed our satellite dish, worrying about health risks. Other broadcasters were opposed to a potential competitor putting up a tower on their mountain.

When things looked bleak in Phoenix, I approached Ed Pastor, a young Maricopa County supervisor who later became a congressman, about helping us get our station on the mountain. He and his friend, Judge Ronnie Lopez founder of Chicanos Por La Causa Inc., requested that our broadcasting colleagues let us get on the mountain. Heavy environmental and aesthetic requirements imposed on us raised the cost of the transmitter building and tower to $1 million, but it was worth it.

Soon, we had put up a transmitter in Denver and were ready to build one in Tucson to fortify our Phoenix station. This caused more trouble and stiffer resistance. The authorities would not give us access to the mountaintop, even though we had a transmitter on the hill. The power was cut off and we thought we were lost, but René Anselmo once again showed his legendary resolve and commitment. He had a diesel-powered generator flown to the transmitter site by helicopter and arranged for regular fuel flights. Our station went on the air and stayed on the air. Once again, we refused to be denied.

It seemed that our business always had an uphill battle to survive and prosper. Thus, the mountaintop held a special significance in our company. Arizona was a symbol that no obstacle, technical or man-made, could keep us from delivering broadcast service to the Hispanic community. We named the Arizona entity Seven Hills Broadcasting, after the legend of Cíbola.

Declaration of War

Our biggest confrontation was not with the television networks but with Spanish radio. Two things started the fighting: the LPTV, which was now a threat to the local stations in the smaller markets, and the fact that we were thinking of starting a radio recording firm as well. Those other station operators must have thought, "My God, here comes the gorilla!"

A small group of station owners from several Southwest states met and decided they were going to get us first. I received a call from someone who had attended. "Danny I've just been to a meeting. *Cuídate, hermano* (take care of yourself). They are going to get you," he said. I called René.

Our attorneys felt the law had been broken. Holding a meeting to discuss "getting" someone in business is considered conspiracy. So we filed a lawsuit, and the war began.

The rival group sent a letter to an U.S. senator from New Mexico. He wrote to the Justice Department charging us with antitrust activities, and to the Federal Communications Commission (FCC) charging illegal foreign ownership.

Of course, the antitrust charges went nowhere. There was no way to monopolize 4 percent of the market, the total Spanish language TV audience. However the FCC, took the allegation of foreign ownership very seriously and started a long, expensive and grueling investigation.

The FCC Hearing

The opposing station owners had charged that Emilio Ascárraga Milmo, who was Mexican, controlled more of the company than his 20 percent share would suggest. The FCC ruled that René, Julie, Nicky and I were beholden to Emilio – that we had an "unnatural relationship."

At the beginning of the yearlong investigation, René, our president said, "We do not have anything to hide. We have not done anything wrong. In fact, we have done a lot of good. So, open your books. Let them talk to anybody and let them see anything they want."

In the end, the investigators found nothing. In fact, we were doing a great job. The FCC official asked, "Would you consider a settlement?" That felt to us like the FCC was slapping our hands so they could justify all the money they had spent.

René exploded: "You have tarnished our names. You have called our reputations into question. Now you are going to clear our names. There will be no settlement. We want a comparative hearing."

To my knowledge, no one else in the history of the FCC had asked for a comparative hearing – where nobody ever comes out whole. Yet, here we were, demanding to be put into one. The FCC official, getting increasingly impatient, said, "Hold that thought, René." He returned with four witnesses and said, "Now say it again, René. Say it." René repeated his expletive-filled demand, so they put us into a hearing.

At the end of the hearing, after days of grueling and treacherous cross-examination, the judge said, "You are not only *not guilty* of doing any thing bad, you are wonderful *exemplary* broadcasters. However, I do not write the law. I only interpret it." He ordered us to restructure the company and separate SIN from SICC. "Restructure" to us meant, "Get rid of the Mexican broadcaster." The 13 SICC stations were ordered transferred to U.S. entities. Emilio Azcárraga Milmo had to go. Two issues now took center stage.

Emilio and René had a long-standing relationship. René had worked for the Azcárraga family for more than 30 years. René's house in Greenwich, Connecticut, now worth millions of dollars, was a gift from Emilio. The FCC's conclusion: "You are beholden to him for that."

I was next. They attacked me on a compensation issue. Very early in my career, Don Emilio had asked me to set up and run his soccer team, the Aztecs, in Los Angeles. I was president of the Aztecs for about two years. He forgot to pay me, and it was a policy of mine never to ask for money. This came out in the investigation. As a result, they felt I was beholden to Emilio. Likewise for Nicky, who also had a close relationship with the Azcárraga family.

I can understand how they came to that conclusion from a purely business standpoint, but this was not your typical business. Our commitment, our fervor and our will to serve and survive had gone far beyond just business. As had become our style, we kept our wagons circled, even when we became profitable.

All of this might look suspicious to the outsider, but to us, this was the secret to our survival. I believe that by the end of our hearing, the administrative law judge understood that and it influenced his decision, thanks to the masterful work of Norman Leventhal, who defended us in all our battles with the FCC.

Hallmark Takes Over

At the time of the FCC hearing, a legal dispute among the partners was winding its way through a Los Angeles court. So, putting the company up for sale was agreed on as a global settlement of both the FCC decision and the partnership lawsuit.

There were many bidders, because SICC's potential in a growing market offered a world of opportunity. The process was traumatic and painful for the partners, straining years of friendships and affection.

Jerry Perenchio, the current chairman and CEO of Univisión, made a preemptive offer of $340 million. The partners, who never seemed to agree on anything, immediately rejected the offer, electing to take our chances with the auction process. Perenchio was very upset and withdrew from the bidding.

As other bidders fell by the wayside, Hallmark Cards, Inc., and First Capital Corp. of Chicago emerged as the most likely bidder at $301.5 million for the SICC licenses and properties; the federal judge approved the transaction. On January 1, 1987, the FCC put SICC and SIN together into what became Univisión, and a new era was born with a new president. Hallmark took control that August. On February 15, 1988, Hallmark became sole owner.

I was the only SICC partner who remained for the transition period. An "office of the president" was formed with Joaquin Blaya as president, Bill Stiles as the Hallmark liaison, and me.

Our Business Family Falls Apart

The sale to Hallmark drove a spike into the heart of our business family. Most of us spoke only a couple of times after that, and some of us never spoke again. I never talked to René after that. He died, and I was never able to tell him how I felt.

The most incredible journey of my life was over, and the end was bittersweet. We had created a great company, but we had all lost a special relationship that had lasted over a quarter of a century.

We had vacationed together. Our children had grown up together and become close friends. Our wives were friends. We had become a family bonded by adversity, legal opposition, physical threats, weddings, births, deaths and a determination approaching fanaticism to protect the rights of our people. We had survived hunger strikes, bombs, threats, gunfire, challenges to our licenses, financial crunches and other obstacles; but we could not survive a letter sent by Hispanic radio broadcasters who felt threatened by our company. We had restructured our company as the judge ordered. The FCC had made us sell our company and had destroyed our family in the process.

I am so grateful that Emilio Azcárraga Milmo called me a few weeks before he died. I told him what a profound effect he and his father had had on my life and that I would always be grateful to him and his family. My last words were

"Puedes contar conmigo, Emilio. Yo estoy contigo hasta el final (You can always count on me, Emilio. I will be with you until the end)." I will always be happy I said those words.

Small Business Owner Again

After a few months as a consultant to Univisión, I went off to do something that would help me decompress. I bought an affiliate in a small California market, Monterey-Salinas, and went back to the basics of building and running a station.

The day-to-day battle to survive at the local level was invigorating. I had missed it more than I ever imagined. We cleaned it up, we brought in new people. And, because of a new investment in our old rival, Telemundo, by my new partner and me, the FCC again ordered me to sell my station.

This time the pain was dulled by the investment in Telemundo. I sold my station to Walter Ulloa, a Hispanic, friend and former assistant at KMEX. He was becoming a fine broadcaster. I knew my puppy was in good hands.

Building Bastion Capital

After the Hallmark deal, I was ready to retire and deal with my midlife crisis. I was 50 years old and I planned to go off and do nothing. Then my son Jim challenged me in the financial arena. So, I set out to learn a whole new business and a whole new vocabulary.

I read everything I could get my hands on. I approached it like a game, much as I did football in high school. I had to take a good look at the venture capital and buyout industry and at myself. What were the most important things to learn? What were my strengths and how could I capitalize on them?

I knew I was not going to become a numbers genius. I would capitalize on my strengths, which are in marketing and the enormous network of people I have built over the years. That is my contribution.

Bill Bron and I founded Bastion Capital as a 50-50 partnership. We believe that investing in Latino and minority companies is wise. Historically, minority funds have not had good records. After the problems in the 1960s, investment funds were started as social experiments. We were once told, "If we get our money back, we will consider ourselves lucky." What kind of investment strategy is that?

We invested $5 million of our own money in addition to our corporate investors' contributions. It comforted them that we were going to keep our eye on the ball. Bastion has $125 million in committed capital, mostly from the largest institutional investors in the country: the California Retirement System; the states of New York, Pennsylvania and Virginia; the Illinois State Teachers Retirement Fund; Packard Bell; and Wells Fargo.

We were the first Latino fund in the United States. Our investors put heavy restrictions on us. We did not finance start-ups. We did not do real estate, gas and oil. We avoided high-tech; that was too risky. The investors wanted to make sure ours was a conservative fund. We invested between $5 million and $25 million dollars in equity in companies.

Other Hispanic funds are coming along. I am now contemplating my next retirement. I want to do something else, something that has never been done before.

One of my goals is to start a company to help inner-city small businesses owned by minorities and women. I would put together a "SWAT" team of young men and women who are specialists in areas such as accounting, marketing, operations and strategic planning. I would make equity investments in small companies and put my team in to straighten the companies out and spruce them up.

This would establish a "farm team" of high-potential start-up and high-growth businesses. It would benefit entrepreneurs by providing quality technical support and growth capital, and it would benefit young professionals by offering them the experience of working with entrepreneurs.

Epilogue

There is much to do and the stakes are high; but from those to whom much is given, much is required. It is our responsibility to ourselves and our community to give, to support and to guide. I believe my parents left a legacy of strength by impressing on me the importance of public service. I hope that this legacy will continue beyond my grandchildren and great-grandchildren. It is true. My mom was right. "Hay que meterle ganas (You have to give it all you've got)."

Notes

[1] According to the Spanish-language Nielsen ratings, Univisión typically claims at least 15 percent of the 20 top rated programs. The network's local affiliate, KMEX, is the single most powerful Spanish-language outlet in the country, blanketing a fifth of the nation's Hispanic market. Its 6 o'clock evening newscast routinely tops others in its time period in the ratings, beating all competitors, English and Spanish. (Cantu, Los Angeles Times 6/22/97)

[2] Nicolás Kanellos, *Handbook of Hispanic Cultures in the United States: Sociology.* (Texas: Arte Público Press. University of Houston, (ed) 1994).

[3] At that time, the FCC's limit was seven stations per owner. That rule has since changed.

CHAPTER FIVE

Nancy Archuleta
One Turnaround After Another

MEVATEC CORPORATION
HUNTSVILLE, ALABAMA

Industry: Technical Services – Aerospace Engineering,
Management Services and Information Technology

Date Started: February 14, 1985

1999 Sales: $63 Million

Percentage Growth for 1999: 25%

Awards, Board Memberships and Accomplishments

2000 Induction to the El Paso Hispanic Chamber of
Commerce Technology Hall of Fame,
Lifetime Achievement for Excellence in Technology.

1999 Administrator's Award for Excellence,
Small Business Administration

1997 National Executive Women's Foundation
Leadership Award

1996 Avon Woman of Enterprise Award,
co-sponsored by SBA

1995 Minority Business Subcontractor of the Year Award,
National Space and Aeronautics Administration (NASA)

The weeping willow in my parents' back yard had beautiful, strong branches. The gnarled limbs close to the trunk made a solid foothold, and the branches were perfectly angled so that I could lean back on them and have a clear view of the sky and the stars. The leaves rustling in the breeze and the warm evening air usually helped to calm me. My weeping willow was my refuge when I needed solace, strength and serenity. It was my place to get away from the chaos of the legacy of dysfunction in my family. Up in my tree, I could lose myself among the stars, weaving dreams of better times. The stars inspired me so much that I often dreamed of becoming an astronomer. At times, my dreams were all I had.

Dad and mom are fourth- and fifth-generation Mexican-Americans. Mom is of Native American descent as well, so one could say that our family has been in this country forever. Both my parents came from dysfunctional families. Needless to say, our home was a whirlwind of emotion. The script had been written and my role cast. I followed the path of dysfunction. As one of the older children, I played my role as the hero child. It was a role rife with responsibility.

Advancing in school was easy for me, so easy that I landed in classrooms with students almost four years older than me. Academically, the challenge was not difficult. But socially, I was not prepared to deal with the peer pressure. Added to the turbulence at home, I was, as the song goes, "Looking for love in all the wrong places." I had my first child at 16. I married the father and dropped out of school. By the time I was 19, I had three children. I now have four children whom I would not trade for anything in the world. But the script had no surprises, and my relationship with their father was terribly abusive.

Abuse is insidious. It erodes a person's sense of self. It kills hopes and dreams. It doesn't take long before suicide seems a better choice than living as an empty shell, constantly questioning your worth, your intelligence and your purpose, and feeling worse all the time. As a result, I spent many years with heavy depression and misguided self-esteem.

The dreams that helped me survive childhood now became nightmares filled with ways to take my life. One fall day, I decided it was time to turn the nightmare into reality. I carefully planned to commit suicide. I remember the day clearly, because I had planned everything to the very last detail. When I think of how close I came to leaving my children, I am overwhelmed with sadness. I don't know how I could have ever thought of leaving them, but in my mind, suicide seemed like my only option.

But that afternoon the good Lord intervened, and I was able to talk myself out of it. I cannot take credit for saving myself. The children were at school. I had the TV on. As I was getting everything ready, I heard the theme music to "As the World Turns." There was something in the music that made me feel as if God was talking to me. "Yes, the world will turn whether you're here or not. Your children will go on living whether you're here or not. But, you are part of it and *you aren't alone.*"

I felt as if I had been taken into space and was looking down at the Earth. I heard my children calling me. I heard their despair as I propelled them into yet another generation of dysfunction. All I could do was cry.

In the days, weeks and months that followed, my mind kept returning to thoughts of suicide, but another part of me sought ways to move forward with my life. It took time, but I set out to plan my future instead of my suicide. First, I had to find a way to support my children. For the next few months I planned every detail of our move. Then one day I put my plan in place. I packed my kids in the car and walked out. I left everything. I even paid all the bills, just so he (my husband) would stay out of my life. I rented a little mobile home and there began turning our lives around. It took a while, but the good Lord hit me "upside the head" and I realized that I had to stop complaining and move forward.

I felt that certain things had to happen in my life so I could fully recover from my ordeal. First, I had to regain and build my self-esteem. I also had to get better at supporting my family financially. When I had dropped out of school at 15, I was one credit away from graduating. I went back to high school and got my diploma. Then I took all kinds of college courses. I started at UCLA and then transferred to New Mexico State University. I never completed college, and that is one of my greatest disappointments, but raising my children was my priority.

Raising four children as a single parent had its challenges. I was divorced for nine years. During that time I learned so much about myself. Then I married a wonderful man who from the very beginning had faith in me and believed I could do anything I set my mind to. He said, "Anybody who could raise four wonderful kids like you have could do just about anything." It took a while for the message to sink in, but it eventually did. I could see all of us moving ahead, becoming whole and building on our past.

It seemed there was never enough money. I made enough money to keep us going, but as the children grew, so did their needs. I started selling insurance in the evenings and weekends to anybody who would listen. I also sold Avon products for a while. Anything I could do to keep the family going, I did. The kids worked, too. They all contributed to keep us together. Hard work never hurt anybody.

Eventually, I went to work for a major insurance company and was soon managing a division. During that time, the division went from being 98th to 30th of 100 divisions in the company. The management at the insurance company was not very supportive. Despite the tremendous growth we experienced, our results – and, most importantly, my achievements – were not recognized. As a result, I soon found myself wondering why I was doing this for somebody else. A friend of mine who also was facing problems at his company asked, "Why don't we do this together?" So we became partners.

Our agency grew steadily. Then, when my partner wanted to move out of the area, he asked if I would buy his share. I did and became sole owner of a relatively successful insurance agency. The agency continued to grow. It was doing well enough that people began approaching me with investment ideas. MEVATEC was one such investment.

MEVATEC

I was asked to be a passive investor in a start-up manufacturing company that would produce circuit boards. I didn't know what circuit boards were, so I asked my husband, who showed me that we had lots of them in our house. So I thought, "Wow, there must be a great market for these." I quickly put up $1,000, signed a joint line of credit for $25,000 and became a 25 percent owner with three other investors. A savings and loan association had endorsed the project, so getting the financing was not difficult.

My plan was to continue to run my insurance agency, and I thought, "We're going to get involved in manufacturing circuit boards. All I have to do is stay at home and clip coupons." It didn't happen that way.

It took me only a few board meetings to figure out that the "idea" man behind all this only wanted to use my name, gender and ethnicity. It soon became obvious that he wanted a front in order to get government contracts as a woman- and minority-owned business. He didn't realize what kind of person he was dealing with. This was not in the cards or the coupons.

Our board meetings were reduced to a routine in which he would say, "You know, I need money for this, that and the other." As we considered his requests, many of them seemed like poor business practices, so we voted against them. For instance, one of the things he wanted to do was to fly first-class to Italy when we didn't even have a manufacturing facility yet.

It wasn't long before he and I became very frustrated with each other. He expressed his dissatisfaction to the other board members, who in turn let me know. Fortunately, I was forewarned. Totally frustrated, I called a board meeting and told him "how the cow ate the cabbage." He yelled and cussed and everything else and said, "Well if you think you can do this better, why don't you?" That was in 1985 and, as they say, the rest is history.

MEVATEC, The Early Years

Fortunately, I wasn't a stranger to building something from nothing. But it took a while to convince the others that a phoenix could emerge from these ashes. They weren't as optimistic as I was but eventually agreed that if they were removed from the debt instruments, they would sell me their stock. For them, it was a no-lose situation. I assumed all the risk. And that is how I became the majority owner.

The only thing left to do in order to get the company going was to draw on my family, friends and community resources. They all agreed to help, and soon we landed our first contract. The local university helped with our training and the required certifications. The state helped out by offering us assistance under the Job Training Partnership Act, and the banker agreed to "help work things out." There have been many angels in my life. I'm just sorry I can't mention them all here.

By early 1987, we had over 40 employees and had landed a major commercial contract to manufacture circuit boards for a pager unit. I invested heavily in equipment and facilities. Words that often come up in conversations about fast growth, such as "growing too fast can be devastating," kept going through my mind. I considered the financial aspects of growth and was satisfied that we could handle it. But I did not consider the effect on the rest of the business and I made one very serious mistake – I stopped marketing to other customers. I based my growth on one customer.

In October of that year, our customer chose to go offshore to manufacture its product, and we were forced to lay off all but a few people. Within a year, it was obvious that I might have to make a very difficult decision and file bankruptcy. The lesson I learned: Never stop selling your company. When I look back on those days, I remember the earth turning and the words, "You are not alone."

Again, my family, friends and associates rallied. Everyone wore several hats. We did some manufacturing and assembly jobs. We even painted doors for a hotel that was opening in our city. We took all kinds of jobs to keep the doors open.

My son read the *Commerce Business Daily* religiously. One day he commented, "I don't know what is going on in Huntsville, Alabama, but the Army is getting and spending lots of money there." He made some contact calls and, soon, our name became known to the Small and Disadvantaged Business Utilization Officer. Her name was Virginia Wright

I do not believe in coincidence. Everything happens for a reason. A few days later, my husband (and biggest fan) could not find the office of the distributor who sold us our solder equipment. He asked for directions in a first-floor office and, as part of conversation, asked what they did. When they told him they worked for the Army, he asked if they knew the company or me. I can only imagine the look on his face when they said that they had been trying to locate me.

Virginia Wright in Huntsville had told them about us. My son's diligence and the timing of my husband's chance encounter put us back on the map. This was the beginning of a strategic alliance that changed our lives forever.

Opportunity is often disguised by challenge. Would I have considered marketing in Huntsville if my company were doing well? Probably not. Manufacturing is a capital-intensive industry. We were never adequately capitalized to enter that market. If these factors had not existed, would I have considered moving into the service industry? Probably not. However, all these "opportunities" forced me to take a close look at what we needed to do to build a successful company.

The company had reached a critical point. We were located in Las Cruces, New Mexico, but we were being offered an opportunity for growth in Huntsville. We had begun as a manufacturing company but were being considered for a major effort in engineering and technical services. I could not ignore the opportunity.

I had three people on our payroll when I left Las Cruces, and I knew I was either going to be in business or I wasn't. I had to make that critical decision. My family was so wonderful, so supportive. They said, "Whatever you decide, we're behind you."

Once again, the Voice said, "You are not alone." We accepted the challenge to build something from nothing, and I was again facing fast growth. It became a priority to have the company establish its identity and its internal structure.

I wish I could have a neat, easy answer for people wishing to grow a company quickly. I don't think a neat answer exists. You have to hire people who are better and smarter than you, and you give them room to grow. You must position yourself for growth. Some planning goes into developing a structure and work processes, but sometimes some of that happens as the result of a mistake and from learning that there was something you missed – you realize the wall is there because you stubbed your toe on it. The other part of growth, the most important part, is learning to listen to and trust your instincts. If you hone your instincts and really listen, you can pull it all together.

MEVATEC Today

MEVATEC provides technical and management solutions to the Department of Defense, primarily the Army, Air Force and Navy. On the commercial side, we have provided services to hospitals and telecommunications companies such as Northern Telecom. We have a very strong Defense Technologies group. We also provide technical and management solutions to customers on activity-based costing and management. That is the cost analysis and research side of the house. The other side of the house creates enterprise software solutions for government and commercial customers.

We have over 400 employees, and if we filled every job we have open right now, we would have closer to 500 people tomorrow. The biggest challenge for MEVATEC is finding qualified people. I understand that companies like ours are currently hiring technical people from developing countries.

When I look at the 50 percent high school dropout rate among Hispanics in some cities, I could just scream. The opportunities are there. We are going to be the largest minority in the United States, but that's not going to mean a thing because we are not controlling the dollars. Our children need access to quality education so they can qualify for jobs like these.

We hired our first employee in 1985. He was a jack-of-all-trades, but mainly he provided engineering support. At that time, I thought MEVATEC would some day have about 40 employees. We immediately started growing. That was where hard work met opportunity and luck. Now we are in a fast-growth mode, and it is not difficult to see us at 1,000 employees in the not-so-distant future.

For the last few years we have been growing at between 40 percent and 75 percent a year. We have established good banking relationships, have an incredibly qualified and dedicated team, and we have stayed abreast of the market. It has been thrilling.

Our future growth will probably come from mergers, acquisitions, and products and services focused in high-growth areas. Part of that growth will come from government contracts, but we will not be totally dependent on them. If we do some strategic mergers and acquisitions, we will focus on companies that already do commercial work.

Employee ownership is very important to our success. We have a stock option plan to ensure that employees have a vested interest in MEVATEC. Everyone who participates in the retirement plan also participates in ownership of the company. I have a very aggressive incentive stock option plan. Employees who are superstars have an additional opportunity to become owners.

We have had the same management team since 1989. There is a lot of stability, and people know that. When employees come here, they know that we will not accept mediocrity because we're an excellence-driven company. We are not always the easiest company to work for, but we get about 30 resumes a day.

I have an open-book management style. It is important to us that employees know exactly what we are doing. They must understand the business side of the business.

We hold quarterly luncheons across the country to meet with employees. Last summer I met with almost every employee to make sure that we were communicating correctly and accurately who we are as a company and how we work. Communication becomes one of the biggest hurdles once you start growing quickly. We try very hard to make sure that communication happens continuously.

Sheet of Music: Management and Communication

One day I found myself listening to two senior people on our staff discussing performance appraisals. I would imagine this conversation happens at least once a year in most companies. Our executive vice president and chief technical officer was telling the vice president of human resources that he did not have time to do personnel evaluations and he thought they were worthless. I suggested that they both go off-site and hash the matter out and come back with an answer.

They came back with a new approach, the Sheet of Music. The rest of management loved it. In the past, we would often say, "Let's get on the same sheet of music," or "Let's make sure we are on the same sheet of music." This multifaceted approach takes advantage of this and has become a very important communication tool at MEVATEC.

Instead of looking at traditional personnel evaluations, I now ask to see a person's sheet of music. Each sheet of music includes a personal employability development plan. Do you want to go to school? Do you want to take classes? Do you want to go to seminars? The employability development plan is really a career development plan. What are you going to do to grow and develop within this organization and not stagnate? What do you enjoy? It is also an in-depth career-counseling tool.

I personally review many sheets across the company to make sure we all have the same goals, objectives and vision. In-depth interviews are not necessary. Instead, the policy is that all employees keep their sheets of music on their desk.

As I visit departments, I may look at the sheets of music to see if they are up to date. Has the person's supervisor reviewed it? Does the person know what the supervisor expects and does the supervisor know what the employee expects from the company? What resources are being spent on the employee? If I ask to see someone's sheet of music and nothing has not been written on it, if it is not full of changes and comments, then it is not being used the way it should. Since our music sheets are communication tools, they are not done once a year. Instead each person's sheet of music should be used on a daily basis.

The resources spent on the employee are an important part of the sheet of music. Investing in employees pays off in many ways. Even if the person leaves the company, we are investing in an individual and, therefore, the community.

I consider every one of our employees to be key. From my perspective, the sheet of music assures that everyone is familiar with the company's vision and goals. I do not want everybody singing a different song. We are all going to sing the same song – it may be a round, different people singing at different levels – but it should be the same song. Otherwise, you just have a cacophony. It has taken a good solid three years for people to understand that we are serious about this, but it is working wonders.

The *Itys*

We say that our company is a company of *itys*. Everything we do has as a point of reference a word that ends in *ity*. Words like qual*ity*, integr*ity*, commun*ity*, and responsibil*ity* are the pillars on which our company was built.

Our emphasis on quality may mean we are not always going to be the cheapest. It means we have to be ready to lose some procurement business, especially if quality otherwise has to be sacrificed. We do not settle for anything mediocre. We do not necessarily offer the lowest prices, but we do offer the best value.

We value integrity. We did not give it a second thought when we returned money to the government after we had finished a contract significantly under budget. We fulfilled the contract and saved over $150,000. I called the customer and said I was de-obligating the money we had saved on the contract. We are ethical and we do not cut corners. Integrity also means we support one another, even when we make mistakes. We are a family, hopefully minimizing the dys-functional side.

We are also very community oriented. We believe very strongly in building our community. Customers know they buy a total package – not just an organization that provides quality services, but a company that invests in the communi-ties in which we have offices. We allocate a certain percentage of our profit every year to helping those who are less fortunate than we are. We use the United Way because it reaches so many. In our community, United Way is a very well-run organization. We also target the Hispanic organizations – especially the college funds. Educational programs are at the top of our list.

We also encourage our employees to work on community projects. We believe that giving to the community has to transcend monetary emphasis. We give our time and expertise as well as our monetary resources. My favorite charities are the shelters for victims of domestic abuse. We have an agency in Huntsville called Hope Place. I have served on its board. I am also very closely affiliated with the National Children's Advocacy Center. Anything that touches children is something I will look at.

Itys were a part of the start-up years as well. I think the two *ity* words that are absolutely indispensable in building a business are agility and adaptability. The entrepreneurial process is like being in a stream of flowing water – you've got to get across by jumping from one rock to another. You'd better jump while you can see the rocks and you'd better be ready to balance yourself because it may be slippery, even though it didn't look slippery when you first jumped. So you have to adapt, but you have to be fast. There is no such thing as "I'll get you an answer tomorrow." Be ready to listen to your gut and then go. I call this phase of growth "Guts and Go."

Another *ity* that played a very important role in my entrepreneurial process was recognizing opportunity. I was looking for growth opportunity when I left Las Cruces and had just three people on the payroll. It was risky, but I could not ignore the opportunity. My customers and contacts are here in Huntsville. The opportunity was here.

One of the things I learned from my mother was tenacity. She was such a good role model. Any time I feel that I can't go on or do something, I just look at my mother and the hardships she encountered in her own life and I know I must move forward. I certainly learned that from her.

God has made sure that humility – another *ity* – stays present in my life. This gift ensures that I keep learning every day from everyone and everything. I have watched myself. When I think I know something well, I stop listening and learning. The next thing I know, I make a mistake. Learning from everyone keeps me at my best. This way I keep growing. I learned humility from my grandmother. She also taught me the importance of having a sense of humor. She was very much a role model in my life.

In my case, the "itys" have been the pillars of success at MEVATEC. They are the pillars that support our culture. It has been the right thing to do, but also the best way to run a successful business. The most remarkable outcome of formalizing our values is that it strengthened our internal culture, and I can easily see that our culture is our competitive advantage.

Culture as Competitive Advantage

In our town and in the business community we are known for our unique culture. MEVATEC is called the "hugging company." I have heard that after a perfectly good job interview, some potential candidates will leave feeling rejected if I do not hug them, because I have a reputation for hugging people. I like the emphasis on people and relationships we have in our organization. We are not expected to be "up" at all times, but we do expect that we will help each other when help is needed.

Our culture is our greatest asset in terms of competitive advantage. Because of our reputation for delivering a quality product, some companies will not bid against us if they know we are bidding. We were the only competitors in the small business arena on an $833 million procurement we won recently. Other life lessons guided me through business ownership as we grew as a family and, later, within my businesses.

Resourcefulness

A story I like to share with my grandchildren is about my grandmother who, for the most part, would not wear her shoes because she did not want to wear them out. After she had worn them for a while and had worn out the heel on one side, she would flip-flop the shoe so she could wear out the other side of the heel equally before she got another pair of shoes. When I asked her why she did that, she answered with a twinkle in her eye, "But I like these shoes. Why shouldn't I do it?"

It wasn't about feeling sorry for herself. It was about having a positive attitude and a sense of humor. My mother also did more with less. We used and recycled everything. When you come from a very poor family, you learn to make do with what you have. You do more with less. When we slaughtered a pig, we used every part of that pig. Nothing was left. This philosophy proved invaluable when MEVATEC was just starting and resources were scarce.

Customer Service

My mother was adamant about leaving things better than she found them. This is from her Native American background. If you take one tree, you plant two. If you borrow one dollar, you repay two. No matter what you do, you always leave it better than you found it. That has been my philosophy in life. It is a major guideline of my business. We are not here to benefit from others, but to provide a benefit to others. This is an important legacy from my family.

At MEVATEC, with each customer, we establish the objectives they would like to meet. Then we try to go beyond what the customer has paid for. We try to do twice as much. We try to save our customers money in the course of providing quality service. To do this we have to be innovative.

Since we are a government contractor, we have had to adapt to the fact that government dollars just do not exist any longer in this community. Our adaptation was to get better. We thought, "The better our quality, the harder and longer they will try to keep us." In the middle of the downsizing, we have been growing.

The $150,000 that we returned to the government was money that needed to find its own good somewhere else. After all, it was my tax dollar as well, and I did not need it. Unexpectedly, it put us head and shoulders above other companies in terms of our approach to doing work. Getting by is not enough. We must do more.

Relationships and Teams

None of us is an island. I learned that from my brother and sisters, and later from my children. My younger sister drowned when she was eight. I nearly drowned trying to save her. We came back from that pain as a family. We made it because we supported each other. We did not use the word then, but we became a team. We worked together and helped each other out.

In business, a spirit of teamwork and camaraderie comes from the little things we do to support and celebrate. We still do the small birthday parties. We send birthday cards. We are only 400-plus employees, but it's still very heartwarming when I go to one of our locations and they are preparing to celebrate someone's birthday. I feel great when I hear someone say, "Yeah, we're going to have our birthday party for so-and-so." We are a family and we support one another.

Mentors

I am not a product of myself. I'm a product of what the good Lord has made and of the role models I have had. Every day I look in the mirror and remind myself not to believe my own hype, so to speak. I hope this makes me a better person, more approachable, more open to ideas. I still have so much to do, and I cannot do it by myself.

I have had a number of mentors throughout my life. In school, teachers always encouraged me to do better. Luckily, a community that helped me by providing attention, encouragement and leadership surrounded me. Business people, college professors and community leaders all took the time to help. Today my life's board of directors, a collection of people I admire profoundly, help guide me as I move forward.

Success

In the early days perched high in my tree, I saw things others did not see. Down on the ground, I learned I had guts – the willingness to take risks – one of my greatest assets. I have found lessons everywhere. I did not choose some of them, but all are now welcome friends. Though some were painful, their challenges represented opportunities. I learned that all these lessons applied to business are a gold mine. Most important of all, I learned that success is much more than leading a high-growth business.

I have had many opportunities to think about success because as MEVATEC has grown, the topic of "success" has comes up more often in conversation. I think this is because people are curious about what success is and how to achieve it. Success is such a relative term. I do not yet think of myself as a success. I believe success is a path, not a journey. I learned early that you always have to keep driving; you always have to keep moving forward. The hero child is never satisfied with any accomplishment. There is a drive to continue working hard to accomplish something new. To some extent, that hero child is still with me, but now we work happily together.

I sometimes consider my major life turnarounds as successes. If they are successes, I can easily attribute them to someone saying, "No way you can do this." When I told my ex-husband I wanted a divorce, he said, "There is no way you can raise these kids by yourself." I answered, "Watch me." Internally I said, "Thank you." In an instant he had given me the will to succeed. My youngest was six months old at the time. I proceeded to raise four children without any child support all those years.

When my supervisor at the insurance company told me I could not grow that division, I did. When he told me I could not manage a group, I became an entrepreneur.

What is success? Winning a big contract, hiring a bunch of people? No. I think success is having your son write a poem about you. It is having your grandkids crawl into your lap and say you have the squishiest, most comfortable lap in the world. Who needs to diet after that? Success is having an employee say, "This is the greatest company I have ever worked for." That to me is how you measure success. Those things are humbling. They are not about money or material things.

Success to me means having four wonderful children who have overcome their own struggles and are leading productive and creative lives. Success is having parents and a family that have grown beyond their shortcomings. Success is having one brother and three sisters who lead fruitful and happy lives. Success is remembering my little sister and knowing that I did all I could to save her.

Success is confronting life's challenges head-on and coming out with a sense of humor and added strength. Success is turning negatives to positives – guts to glory. When I look back at the results of all the hardship, the benefits have been the development of tremendous survival skills – intuition, creativity, leadership, vision and persistence. It is a great, wonderful thing to grow from a caterpillar to a butterfly.

Epilogue

It may be hard to believe, but that grand weeping willow almost died. It was down to a stump. On one of my recent visits to New Mexico, my father took my hand and led me to the stump and – miracle of miracles – it is coming back.

I may not have gone to the stars physically, but my products are on the space shuttle through a contract with NASA. I currently serve on an advisory committee to NASA Administrator Dan Golden. It is a great source of pride and accomplishment. So, I may not have become an astronomer, but the stars still mean a lot to me. My children, my parents and my family as a whole are my greatest sources of pride and accomplishment. Today, I realize that while "As the World Turns" played, I received a message that I was part of a grander scheme than I could have imagined. I have learned about the importance of relationships, family, humor and hard work. My son wrote a poem for my latest birthday, and it means the world to me.

Reach for the Stars

Atop the tree she gazed up high
To see the stars so bright.
In worn-out shoes and hand-me-downs
She dreamed 'most every night.

She dreamed of space and rocket ships
And places far away.
She closed her eyes and prayed to God
To take her there some day.

Her friends would laugh and joke out loud
"You'll never reach the stars."
But she'd just smile and walk away
With a dream tucked in her heart.

Now the years have passed and she's grown up
And the dream still lingers on.
And though it's true she may not fly
She still has proved them wrong.

For that little girl has reached the stars
On that you sure can bet.
For her brave heart travels far
On a ship called MEVATEC.

With all my love, your son Gabe

Dr. Tom Velez
Leadership From the Streets of the South Bronx

COMPUTER TECHNOLOGY ASSOCIATES (CTA), INCORPORATED
ROCKVILLE, MARYLAND

Industry: Information Systems Solutions
Started: October 1979
Revenue: $100 Million

Awards, Board Memberships and Accomplishments

1979 Founded CTA

1996 Entrepreneur of the Year Award
from Ernst and Young

1960 - 1969 Multiple NASA Awards
for Technical Achievements

1950 Carnegie Hall Performance as Solo Violinist

VIVACE, INCORPORATED
NEWPORT BEACH, CALIFORNIA
(SPIN-OFF FROM CTA)

Industry: Internet Based Applications for E-Government
Started: 1999
Revenue 2000: $45 Million
Revenue 1999: $20 Million

This memory is clear. I was 12. My father and I woke up early and got ready for a long day. My family never owned a car. We could not afford to take a taxi, so it would be public transportation all the way. I carried my violin and an overnight bag as we walked down the stairs at the Grand Concourse subway station in the South Bronx and headed to Penn Station. From there we took a train to Connecticut and then a bus into town. We then walked three miles to a mansion called *Su Casa* (your house), where I would perform for guests that evening on my violin. The next day we repeated this sequence in reverse. Each trek took about six hours.

My father was dressed as he always did, in suit and tie. In my lifetime, I can hardly remember a time when my father did not wear a tie. He was a short-order cook in midtown New York City. Every morning he put on a suit and tie, changed into his whites at work and changed back at the end of the work day. Even in the grittiest of New York summers, my dad always changed into his suit and tie to come home.

I assumed a Latino family owned the mansion. But a non-Latino family greeted us when we arrived. As my dad and I settled in, the sheer beauty of the place overwhelmed all of my senses – it was a beautiful, beautiful home – clean, orderly and quiet. It was my first experience with a bath/shower, but I liked the bed most of all – the clean smell was intoxicating. The linens were crisp with starch. I wanted *Su Casa* to be *mi casa* (my house). I told Dad I wanted a house like this. His response was delivered with the conviction of a loving father who *also* wanted this for his son. He said, "If you want to live like this, go to school and study hard." So I did.

My father, Amadéo Jesús Velez, was born in Ecuador and was a self-made man. He completed only the earliest grades in school and taught himself to read and write, first in Spanish and later in English. He was essentially a wise man of integrity who took every opportunity, even as we walked the sad streets of the South Bronx, to teach me about honesty, hard work and, of course, education. I do not know where he got his wisdom, but I am blessed that he shared it with me.

He became an American citizen in his late 50s. In the course of studying for citizenship, he discovered Thomas Jefferson. Jefferson's idea that "with freedom comes responsibility" struck a chord with my dad, who became immersed in reading everything he could find about Jefferson.

I have only a sketchy picture of his early years before he emigrated to the United States. He was a musician and a horseman, a proud man who dressed well and had impeccable manners. He ran away from home at age 13 and entered the Ecuadorian army, which was fighting a 100-year war with Peru over territory. He was hurt while in the army and later contracted malaria. Eventually, he ended up in Santiago, Chile, and worked on ships that brought produce to the United States. It must have been horrendously dirty and dangerous work. On one trip, my dad applied for a permanent visa in the United States and stayed. Initially, he worked in the Brooklyn Navy Yard as a welder but, weakened by the malaria, he left that job and became a cook. He was a simple guy with a lot of caring and love to give.

My dad and the streets of the South Bronx were my life and leadership mentors. Music tied it all together and made my education possible. Many years after that day at *Su Casa*, I started a company that would make tangible my vision of an exciting place to work. Yet, one consistent and unexpected challenge colored the in-between years. Each time I heard my father's voice saying, "Go to school, study hard." In the end, my father's advice made all the difference. Today I would not change a thing – challenges and all.

Music and School

I guess one of my father's goals was to get me out of the South Bronx. He signed me up for violin lessons when I was five, as a special inner-city student at the Manhattan School of Music, a very reputable institution. By the time I was 11 or 12, I was very good. I was not great, but I was good enough to start winning small contests that the New York Music Education League sponsored for children.

I was also good enough to win a part-time scholarship to the Juilliard School of Music when I had the opportunity to study orchestral conducting, a fabulous experience that would serve me well as a future CEO. Anyway, I occasionally won student contests, and once I won the opportunity to perform at Town Hall. It does not exist any more, but in those days it was an alternative to Carnegie Hall.

I played there in a student concert as a soloist. My performance of Mendelssohn's Violin Concerto in E minor was a success I will never forget. My nervousness, the painstaking hours of practice and fear of failure disappeared the moment I began playing. I have never seen my father, sitting in the first row, so proud. The pride he felt, watching his son in the Connecticut mansions of the very wealthy who sponsored the Sunday musicales, carried him through any embarrassment he might have felt about his job as a short-order cook in the inner city.

In high school, I moved from playing classical to jazz violin. By 15, I had a cabaret license, was a member of the musicians union and was playing with a group called The Playboys Four. We had a phenomenal run of successes playing in the Catskills in the summer and the city clubs the rest of the year. This started in my senior year in high school and continued all through college and graduate school. It was a nice way for me to make money. It paid for school, books and tuition and at the same time gave me time off so I could study. I was very lucky. That music career really played a big role in my being able to finish school.

Lessons in Entrepreneurship and Leadership

My father's lessons, the comprehensive curriculum in leadership offered gratis by the streets of the South Bronx and my musical training helped me start and build Computer Technology Associates, Inc. These sources of instruction meshed in interesting ways, sometimes overlapping, other times supplementing. One thing is true: They kept me moving forward when it would have been easier to stay put.

Pay for Performance

Once, when I was still young enough to be holding my father's hand while crossing city streets, dad pointed out a group of people lined up in the street outside a tenement building waiting for the mail carrier. He told me some of these people were waiting for relief checks but also had jobs. They fooled the system by having two names and a social security number for each name. He believed they wanted something for nothing and were getting money without earning it. His integrity was violated to the point of anger. He often said, "Only take what you earn." This meant, "Don't take something you didn't earn and don't deserve." Today, this applies to our employees. I started a very strong pay-for-performance program at CTA as a result of my father's lessons.

"Earn your pay" also applies to our clients. I believe that a value system is only as good as the mechanisms you create to implement it. At CTA, we have a "No-Questions-Asked Warranty." If you do not like the service we provide, you get your money back or we will continue working until we get it right.

A short story. When we started CTA, we worked with prime contractors. Primes, as we call them, secure large contracts from the government and at times subcontract portions of the work to smaller companies like CTA. Once we received a time-and-materials subcontract from a prime to do a human-factors analysis. As a subcontractor, we had to go through the prime for clarification of the requirements. Though we tried to understand the requirements, in the end the customer did not like the analysis but paid the prime, who in turn paid us for the hours expended on the effort. At a subsequent internal review of this project, I learned that we had been paid approximately $53,000 for the effort and that the ultimate customer would not be using our work. In effect, he planned to discard our analysis.

I thought about this overnight. Next morning, I called the prime's manager and said we would be returning his payment for our services, despite the fact that there was no legal obligation to do so. The prime sent the check back to us. "We don't want your check," they said. "We've made profit on your effort, and there is no obligation for a refund."

I insisted. The government, in this case the Air Force, asked about the check. The prime told them we had insisted on returning the money because we had not understood the requirements of the project. This created additional work for the Air Force, which had to devise a new capability: to accept money. To my knowledge, our refund set a precedent at the Air Force's operations in Colorado Springs.

An interesting and unexpected outcome resulted from this decision: It created tremendous internal pride in the company. I was further surprised when I heard directly from the Air Force. They wanted to deal directly with companies that lived by this value system. I believe that the tens of millions of dollars of business from the Air Force we enjoyed over the subsequent years were due in large measure to that $53,000 refund.

Whether it was my father finding and returning two bucks in the subway station because "it did not belong to us" or pointing out unscrupulous behavior, he was clear: "Earn your pay. Keep only what you deserve."

Developmental Feedback

As I said earlier, I started violin lessons at the age of five. Dad sat through every lesson until I entered the Manhattan School of Music at nine. He observed the teachers. Once a teacher slapped my hand because I played a wrong note. My dad, with his demeanor of respect and self-control, told the teacher to show me how to do it right instead. After every class and across many teachers, my father pointed out which teachers were better than others and why. Today, despite how hard it is, I try to give feedback much as Dad did, with respect and caring. Some people call this "tough love."

I believe that effective, constructive criticism takes a commitment of caring, which is uncommon in corporate America. Yet, there is no doubt in my mind that this type of commitment is essential for the continued growth of our creative and talented high-technology leaders. Years ago I began noticing that occasionally talented people would enter what I call the "Land of the Living Dead," where their progress in the company seriously stalled. They did not get an expected promotion or bonus; they felt this was unfair and not reflective of their perceived performance or potential, but planned to stay in this state of dissatisfaction.

The person who is having this type of difficulty is now asked to join "the club" and agrees to select a mentor – someone he or she trusts – from among the senior executive staff. That senior level executive is tasked to coach the "living dead" person for six months, an expensive but worthwhile investment. Feedback is provided on a daily basis – after meetings, before and after major events and when dealing with technical and personnel issues. The feedback is brutally honest: "Everybody thinks you're bullshitting them," or "Nobody believes you."

This program, though seldom used, has produced exceptional executives for CTA and for other high-technology firms. It is a source of deep pride when I hear from other organizations that are benefiting from the technical or leadership contributions of people who are now "among the living" again.

In retrospect, it is not a difficult or complicated program. The hardest part is taking a person aside and starting the process. In the South Bronx, difficulty in confronting a tough call or marginal play is not an issue, especially if you want to play and walk the streets. It is one of the ways one gains respect. Feedback is an essential tool for a business owner, but it takes commitment and caring – much like my father showed me. It also takes some guts, as the streets showed me.

Customer service

My dad always did what he said he was going to do. When I was six years old, kids were beating me up after school for my lunch money. When my father heard this, he told me that he would be there the next day, even though it was not his day off. As important as losing a day's pay was, he showed up! I cannot remember a time when he let me down.

Most people do not intend to give their word and then break it. However, the fact is they let it happen somehow, through unforeseen events, unexpected delays and so on. On the other hand, individuals who take their word extremely seriously and who rarely fail to deliver are trusted, as I trusted my father. The same is true of companies.

Companies that are reliable suppliers, even when it is hard or expensive, are attractive. The market places high value on that particular attribute, probably because it is rare. Keeping your word is a tremendous asset to any business. Not keeping your word can destroy a business, especially a start-up business.

Leadership

Leadership in the South Bronx is honest, sometimes brutally honest. A political presence in that arena means zero. Leadership is created by personal power and not by assignment. There is no place to hide and nothing to lie about. You live the life you live. You are who you are. I have thought about how leadership happens on the streets. A gang member becomes the leader. No one assigns that role. He doesn't attend a leadership seminar. One kid rises from among the group and just becomes the boss – the leader.

Half-court basketball shows how this happens in inner-city sports. On days when the weather allows, those wanting to play hurry to the playground and line up. The first to arrive gets first chance to throw from the goal line.

The first two people to make a basket from the goal line are the captains. In alternating fashion they select their teams, starting with the best players. By the end of the summer, everyone knows the skills of each player. Those who show talent lead and play most often. They win. It does not occur to anyone to complain about "why I didn't make the team" or, in corporate terms, "why I didn't make vice president."

Music and Leadership

I believe music has played a large role in the success of CTA, much larger than my legal degree or my Ph.D. in math.

The parallels between music and business have always been interesting to me. The fundamental elements of music – innovation, expression, discipline, teamwork and a passionate energy for excellence – are now written as the fundamentals of great businesses.

As in business, music is the kind of venture that requires continuous vigilance – you have to play every aspect of every note just right. It's unforgiving. The slightest mistakes are noticed and rarely forgotten. This can describe business as well. Every aspect of a business must be performed well – clients must be satisfied, employees fulfilled and profits returned to investors. Business is a discipline. It gets better with practice, is complex and must succeed in every aspect. Business is also unforgiving. If you make a mistake, all your customers, investors and employees know it and rarely forget.

Creating music and leading are related. I may not be able to describe the connection exactly, but it is very strong. Part of it is a feeling. I describe this feeling as the passion of leadership. I "felt" leadership for the first time during my course in conducting at Juilliard. It is not just about waving a stick in front of a bunch of people. The stick is almost irrelevant. You can stand and look at an orchestra and lead them. Leadership, like conducting, is about who you are and how you create harmony and intensity. People often use the word "synergy" to describe the phenomenon of creating value (or beauty) that goes beyond what is possible separately from talented individuals.

There is a marvelous training film on leadership based on Ravel's "Bolero." It is a tape without words. Zubin Mehta is the featured conductor. No single instrument carries the melody in "Bolero." Instead the melody is the harmony of instruments playing together. Mehta's job is to create an extraordinary result by the integration of a broad spectrum of skills and personalities. This is precisely the role of a CEO.

An experienced orchestra and conductor can take about a minute to recognize each other's nonverbal signals.

Conductors have walked on stage, never having conducted a particular orchestra before, and given world-class performances. That is leadership.

The most common language on the planet is physical expression. Certain things about expression and body language are universal. It may be a frown from the conductor who wants more intensity from the players, a shaking of the head, an expression of elation or the way his hands go way up in the air as if he is about to jump out of his pants. But each musician immediately translates it into a specific action. This is honest communication. This is teamwork. This is performance.

Leadership, like conducting, is not about knowing how to play each instrument like a virtuoso, or even being a competent musician. Most conductors agree that each musician plays his or her instrument better than the conductor could ever play it. Most leaders know that their staffs have more technical capability than they do; the longer you are a leader, especially in technology, the truer this statement becomes.

Leadership, like conducting, is the non-technical glue that coordinates and harmonizes a company. The intensity comes through values, through pride and through experience. Without any evidence other than my own feelings, I think music in this context and with these rules has played a large role in my success as a leader.

School and More School

I was in college when I realized that being a Hispanic was a problem. I thought that a baccalaureate degree in mathematics and a grade point average of nearly 4.0 would help secure jobs. I started looking for a job as a software programmer in my senior year. At that time, companies used a standard Programmer's Aptitude Test (PAT) as an entry requirement for all software developers. It is a very tough test: a timed test on which the objective is to finish as much of it as possible within the allotted time. No one was expected to complete it.

In the ensuing months, I interviewed with many companies – all the big oil companies, all the insurance companies and all the banks in New York. Many had articles in New York newspapers saying that they were looking to maintain and grow their programming departments. It seemed there were plenty of job opportunities, but I could not find a job.

I went to so many job interviews that eventually I could finish the PAT before time ran out, causing the examiners to become suspicious of possible cheating. I must have taken that test at least 50 times. But the bottom line was that I could not get a job.

A recruiter suggested changing my last name, realizing that the real impediment to employment was my heritage rather than my qualifications. I did not have the heart to change my last name. I could never face my father if I did. I am glad I didn't.

My dad's advice was to continue schooling, so I went back to the university to get a master's degree. In two years, while still performing as a musician for income, I earned a master's in math and computer science, with a perfect 4.0 GPA, and applied for a job with the government at any agency hiring entry-level programmers. I was still unable to get any offer of employment!

Instead of getting seriously angry, giving up and reconciling myself to the life of a mediocre musician, I prepared to apply for a doctoral degree. One day, without any action on my part, all that changed. NASA initiated an affirmative action program for Hispanics and African-Americans. On my application, they saw a Hispanic with an "A" average from a technical graduate school. NASA offered me a one-year position, sight unseen, and offered to pay for graduate school if I did well and became a full-time employee. I accepted without an interview, not caring that the job was in the state of Maryland, which seemed like the Deep South to me at the time, and that the offer was only for one year. I needed a job!

Professional Life at NASA

I finally got out of the Bronx. I purchased a used car and drove to Maryland to work at NASA's Goddard Space Flight Center. I left the Bronx for a place where towns had names like Hyattsville and Greenbelt. Let me tell you about cultural trauma! I could not believe I was doing this. I almost turned my car around and drove back to the Bronx.

However, given the opportunity, I grew quickly within the technical community at Goddard. My job was to build software in support of research and development activities during the most exciting years in NASA's history. I began as an entry-level programmer and developed my skills on the job with the caring help of my supervisors. As my skills matured, it was sheer pleasure working, doing research and co-authoring articles with professors from Yale, MIT, Stanford and Harvard.

During this period of my development, I co-authored about 40 or 50 papers and wrote parts of several books. This work created opportunities for me to develop teams of engineers dedicated to performing leading-edge research in support of NASA's missions. I went up the management ladder by performing as a leader before I got the title, a valuable lesson from the streets of the South Bronx. I believe my father was right the discipline of my schooling and musical training gave me the power to compete with the best, to work on important programs and to prepare for the next challenge.

I loved working for NASA. I would have done it for free. That kind of excitement is rare. I also felt that way about playing music. Yet, despite how much I enjoyed working for NASA, I knew that in the end I wanted to do something else.

Starting CTA

I started CTA because I wanted to create, to some degree, a similar kind of feeling of the excitement for relevant, meaningful work that I had experienced at NASA. I wanted to create the kind of professional excitement that employees would want to tell their grandkids about.

Goddard had that kind of work. We stayed there, not because of pay but because we wanted to be part of a big picture. We wanted to play a role in making a difference on a national scale. In that kind of culture, a company does not have to worry about attrition. It is truly amazing.

CTA Today

At CTA, we strive do the kinds of things within the information technology marketplace that have national importance. It is such a blessing to have that excitement as part of my life today.

My company has had many lives since we started. I have started companies and spun them off, bought companies and sold them. Right now, the company has nearly 1,000 employees.

We provide information technology solutions and consultants to federal, state and commercial clients. That means we do software-oriented work and are involved in the development of computer networks in support of the businesses of our clients. We do everything from helping the government buy new systems to building and supporting them.

For example, we are helping the federal government develop advanced information systems for hospitals. This is a technology that would allow patient medical records to be transferred between hospitals and medical practitioners quickly, securely and reliably, using Internet-based technologies.

We are also working with the Defense Department's command and control systems. Our roots are in aerospace and the defense industry. The benefit of this is that over the years, we have developed a strong methodology for building reliable software that we apply to a broad spectrum of clients.

Now more than ever, we are engaged in a rapidly growing part of the market, which involves developing, supporting, maintaining, installing and upgrading software.

The software business is a very tough business. Software is hard to build, and it is hard to test and maintain. It always costs more than it should. Software has been the Achilles' heel in many of the large systems that governments have tried to deploy, whether it is the baggage handling system at the Denver airport or a major upgrade in air traffic control. Those two examples have cost the state and federal governments literally millions of dollars, with marginal return.

It is a tough business with lots of opportunity. The industry is global, and it is moving to more Internet operations and to increased integration of its various components. There are opportunities for companies like ours to exploit that market with exceedingly solid engineering capabilities. Our advantage is our technical experience base. It is a core competency.

The Year 2000 bug is a good example. The next important part of our business will be the euro, as the European market goes to a common currency. All of the software – things like financial accounting, payroll and customer relations – will have to reflect the Euro as opposed to or in addition to local currency, and that is a big information technology problem. Some of the people who forecast trends in this industry estimate that conversion to the euro will cost even more than the problems associated with the Year 2000 bug, which in itself is estimated to have cost between $600 billion and $1 trillion.

Companies globally are employing electronic commerce technology to increase operational efficiency – for instance, to decrease the response time to customer demands and to improve supply chain management. The demand for power-ful, networked computer systems with supporting software, specifically adapted to the needs of a particular market seg-ment, will therefore increase.

CTA is a market-driven company. We follow the market. We also follow technology, and we adapt new technologies to the needs of our customers. Years ago I was involved in the research side. I have learned that there are many bright young people out there – all about 23 years old. They become people like Steve Jobs and Bill Gates. They dream up things in their garages. Competing with those minds is not as pro-ductive as working with them. Working with them means leveraging what they have developed and applying it to our market.

That is our strength. We listen to our customers and know our market. When we think that one of those new ideas can work well for our customers, we bring it to them in a way that provides solutions. That may mean maturing the tech-nology and then customizing it. This is what CTA does best.

Growth

I cannot say simply that we want to be a large company. Large is always in the eye of the beholder, like love or beau-ty. When I look up I see EDS, I see Cap Gemini, and I see IBM Systems Solutions. I see Kean, Arthur Andersen Consulting, and Price Waterhouse. All these companies are much larger than CTA. Each has at least 10,000 employees, some more. Their sales are over $1 billion. Some of them are multibillion-dollar businesses. These are our competitors. All these com-panies do what we do.

Our goal is in the next two years is to be a profitable com-pany with revenues of about $250 million. We have very nice accounts. We have major states: Nebraska, Kansas, Texas, Iowa, and California. We are currently working with major national airports. We are doing LAX, Orlando and Boston and the New York Port Authority, which includes La Guardia and JFK. We have government contracts with the Navy, the Air Force, the FBI and the FAA. Our commercial clients include companies such as Wells Fargo, Dannon, Norrell and Centacor. With our record of accomplishments and our success in growing, an IPO may be possible in the near future.

Epilogue

When I look back I say, "Thank God those companies rejected me when I was applying for all those jobs." I was driven to go to school because I just did not want to be rejected any more. My father played such an important role. He made school such an important part of my inner being that my natural reaction was, "I've got to work harder. I have to get more degrees. I have to get better grades. I've got to get more schooling." Going off into the sunset, becoming a bum or a gangster would have been very easy. I was one of those kids who – if it had not been for my father – would probably be a drug addict and in jail today. My father would not let that happen, and he started early.

After I started CTA and before my father died in 1986, one of the miracles of my life happened. He took me to Ecuador. I had never been to Ecuador. He took me to his mountain village, San Cristóbal. The village lay outside a town called Cuenca. I saw then who he was. He was the son of a proud mountain Indian. My father was half Quechua, a people from the highlands of the Andes Mountains. I remember he put his arm around the shoulders of one of his friends and said, "This is my son. Let me tell you about my son." I thought, "This is my father. Let me tell you about my father."

CHAPTER SEVEN

Teresa McBride

*Family Values in the
Game of Business*

McBRIDE, INC.
ALBUQUERQUE, NEW MEXICO

Industry: Computer Technology Solutions

Date Started: October 15, 1986

Revenue: $205 Million

Rate of Growth: 33%

Awards, Board Memberships and Accomplishments

2000 Board Member, The New Alliance

2000 Board Member, Federal Reserve Bank-Denver

1997 Avon Woman of Enterprise

1993 Woman of the year, Mexican American
Opportunity Foundation

1990 Small Businessperson of the Year SBA

A s a child I loved visiting Aunt Toñita and Uncle Clemente, my dad's aunt and uncle, in the small town of Cubero in the mountains of New Mexico. Around Christmas one year, I found mistletoe near their house. I asked my dad, "Can I bring some home with me?" He said, "Sure."

So, I took a bunch of it and put it in the back of the truck. Back in town, I bought red ribbon, cut the mistletoe into small bunches, tied the ribbon around them and sold them at the post office. I made $90 dollars that day and convinced my dad I needed more mistletoe. I guess I have been an entrepreneur all my life.

Family Values, Business Values

My family means everything to me. My values, preferences and interests developed early within our very close extended family. My family provided an environment that encouraged growth and development. Indeed, I can trace most of my values to a specific conversation with a specific person, in a specific place and time.

I remember the family stories the best. These were stories about the many generations of relatives who struggled to survive incredible hardships. From them, I learned about life, people and business. I learned about hard work, integrity, leadership, relationships, tolerance for differences and integrating all aspects of life. More importantly, I learned that power and energy come from inclusion and not exclusion. I learned to explore and not to be afraid to try new things.

These family lessons form the foundation of the way I lead my life, my company and the people at McBride, Inc. It is a fiscally conservative company that has experienced tremendous growth. However, we are not conservative when it comes to how we manage people. A very diverse group of people work at McBride – all ages, all races and a larger percentage of women than in most companies. Visitors will comment, "I've never seen this many women in a room," or "I've never seen people from this many cultures in a company."

Of all our accomplishments, I am most proud of this and the values around associate (employee) relations. Although we have people from all walks of life, they work well together as a team. Their dedication, energy and hard work translate into a tremendous competitive advantage. They allow us to play in an industry of giants.

My Early Years

I was born in Grants, New Mexico, a mining community of about 4,000 or 5,000 people at that time. Grants sits at the base of Mt. Taylor, one of the highest mountains in New Mexico. The town was named after the manager who ran the railroad camp in the 1800s.

I was the youngest of three children and the only daughter. My father loved his family and enjoyed sharing life with others. When I was a little girl, the one-and-a-half-hour drive to Albuquerque took most of the day because of all the stops we made to visit family and friends on the way.

My Father and Mother

According to our records and family tree, my father's family came from Spain in the 1600s and has lived in this area of New Mexico for many generations. The McBride brothers had emigrated in 1772 from Belfast, Ireland. A descendant later settled in New Mexico, a province of Mexico in the 1800s, and started a family.

My father, Eduardo Salomón McBride, left Grants in the 1930s when he was 17 and became a seaman in the Merchant

Marine. As a seaman during World War II and into the 1950s, he traveled all over the world, his stories about all the places he had visited opened up the world to me.

His attitude toward life and adventure made access to that world possible for me. He would say "Teresa, you can do anything you want to in life. If you set your goals, develop your skills and then work hard, it doesn't matter what it is; you can achieve it." He truly believed in people, and those who knew him well always tell me that I am like my father in the faith I have in others.

My mother, Dora Lee Bustamante Gonzalez, was named after the midwife who delivered her. She was born in Loving, New Mexico, just outside of Carlsbad. As a young woman, her parents had moved to the United States after both her grandfathers were killed in the Mexican Revolution. Their family ranches were looted and repossessed. She moved to Albuquerque and lived with her Aunt Consuelo, her father's sister.

My mother is the picture of calm, and I learned about serenity and perspective from her. Her calmness seems to come from a profound trust in God, life and people. It gives her a presence of quiet dignity. She never worries about details, though she is a very detail-oriented person.

Her calmness is especially noticeable in frustrating moments. I learned early from her that picking battles carefully and keeping calm in the face of frustration is very good strategy. For instance, when someone is blatantly prejudiced, no matter what anyone might say, that person will not change. In such cases, remaining calm and keeping perspective is the best option. This does not mean being quiet and tolerating this type of rudeness; it means being respectful in the exchange of ideas.

My parents met and married when my father returned to New Mexico. My parents were a great team; they believed in each other and in their children. My parents were resourceful. They did all their own veterinary work on our ranch, as well as plumbing and electrical work. In those days, if you needed something done, you figured it out how to do it and did it. Even though we were not rich, we had everything we needed. We had an abundance of love – expressed in time, energy and lots of lessons.

Luis McBride

Everyone in town called my grandfather *Don* Luis. He was a tall man with piercing blue eyes and sandy hair, born in 1880. As a family patriarch, everybody respected him. When he walked into a room, everyone stood up and put out their cigarettes. He was the owner of a bar on Route 66, as well as a dance hall, barbershop, garage and gas station.

He supported his sisters, Toñita and Beneranda, because that was his duty. He also helped the rest of the town with loans and gifts. When his safe was opened after he died, it was filled with IOU notes that went back 40 years. The safe alto contained a book of poetry he had written.

Clara Serna McBride

I lived with my Grandma Clarita, my father's mother, for the first six years of my life. Her house was just a short trail away from my parents' house. We did not live in a neighborhood; we lived in the middle of town. We did not have neighbors in any direction. We had only businesses.

Grandma Clarita was born in 1886, the 20th of 22 children. Her father's first wife had 11 children before she passed away, and his second wife had another 11 babies.

I had a wonderful time living with my grandmother. I remember that time of my life vividly. I can still see her and remember her aroma when I close my eyes. A wood-burning stove heated the house. We frequently worked outside and chopped our own wood. We had chickens, and she often killed one for dinner. She had a green thumb and grew all kinds of vegetables and many fruit trees. I helped her gather fruits and vegetables for our meals; we also did a great deal of canning.

I spent my formative years with her, and then she was taken away. Because I missed her, I played and replayed my memories of our times together. If she had lived, I probably would not have played those mental tapes so often. In this way she became a permanent fixture in my mind.

Because she was older, and I was her youngest grandchild, I was the center of her world. We spent every moment together. Grandma and I talked for hours every day about life. We did not have a television and I don't even remember a radio. She taught me that every single day you have the opportunity to do something special for someone. When you do not, you have lost a precious opportunity. It was important to her to do the right thing at all times, because nothing was more important than life.

My grandmother lived across the street from the train station and she fed the hobos every day. Because it was so natural for her to help others, I thought they were supposed to be at her house. She never made it seem like she was doing anything out of the ordinary, and she always treated them with respect. Years after she was gone and long after the train station was closed, townspeople still remembered her. I learned compassion and caring for everyone from my Grandmother Clarita.

My parents followed her tradition. Every year, my father held Thanksgiving dinner at his restaurant for anyone who did not have a place to go. My parents made people feel like our place was where they were supposed to be. Though my father passed away in 1977 when I was 14, people today still tell me how they miss him. My father provided a sense of security for me that was hard to regain after his death.

Grandma also taught me about business. Years earlier, from 1930 to 1948, on the same street as my grandfather, she had had her own small café called the Sunshine Café. She served green chili, beans and sopapillas. Again the themes of respect for others and doing the right thing emerged, this time as I was told stories about running her business.

We were a family of entrepreneurs; there are many entrepreneurs in the Hispanic community. You do what you have to do make ends meet. It is what you do to survive. Growing up, I accepted entrepreneurship as the norm.

My grandmother's ancestors were also from Spain and lived in New Mexico long before it became a state. My father's parents never felt like they were foreigners, although their first language was Spanish and they spoke limited English, because their families had been in the community for many, many generations.

Andrés Gonzalez

My grandfather on my mother's side, Andrés Gonzalez, also came to this country as a child. His father was killed during the revolution. The revolution had become a problem, so my great-grandfather sent his wife and five younger children to Texas to live with friends and relatives. Shortly thereafter, my great-grandfather was singled out, blindfolded and executed in front of his two oldest sons – my mother's father, Andrés, and his brother Manuel. The boys feared for their lives, so they left on foot to locate their mother and siblings. My Grandfather Andrés was 11 years old when he left Mexico.

He was a big man. He had some German in him, so he had light skin and green eyes. Because he only spoke Spanish, he was barred from going into certain businesses. My uncle remembers a time when he wanted a toy in the window of a shop. My grandfather went to someone else's house and sent them to go buy it because he could not go into the store.

Andrés died when I was one year old, so I learned about him from family stories. I learned that his family came first.

He was very close to his wife and treated her very well. They were a team and worked their farm together. When my grandfather went to town to sell his produce and animals, he always brought back a present for my grandmother. I learned about compassion from him, and that it is all right to love unconditionally.

I inherited a sense of trust from him. I believe that people deserve chances. My managers say that I do not give up on anybody. I guess this is true, but I have found that this works out more times than not.

Eliser Gustamante Gonzalez

My grandmother Eliser Gustamante's family knew my grandfather's family in Mexico and also took part in the Mexican Revolution. She remembers hiding in a hole in the ground with her mother and siblings because revolutionaries came to their ranch to steal their food and anything else they had. One day her father was executed without warning. The rest of the family waited until dark and left the ranch on foot. Grandmother, her mother, and her brothers and sisters moved north. After they came to the United States, they encountered a lot of prejudice. She told stories that in Texas, southern New Mexico and along the border, they could not eat in restaurants or go into certain stores.

Language became Grandmother Eliser's symbolic defiance against the lack of acceptance she felt in her new country. Though she lived in the United States for 70 years, she only spoke Spanish – or I should say refused to speak English. When my Grandfather Andrés Gonzalez died in 1963, and because Grandma Eliser had never learned to drive, I drove Grandma to some of her doctor's appointments and shopping. I teased her because she pretended not to speak a word of English when we were out in the community. For example, she would say, "*¿Que dicen? No entien-*

do" (What did they say? I don't understand). But she had no problem understanding "Bonanza" or "Gunsmoke."

She was a proud woman, the mother of eight. Respect was very important to her and our family. It was very hard on her when her family was shown a lack of respect because they were Mexican. Running a household of eight children is like running a business. She was always kind and patient with her many grandchildren. My mother is calm like grandmother.

My grandmother and her daughter or Tila, short for Otilia, moved in with my parents right after her husband died. Tila had Down syndrome. All of us grandchildren painted or played dolls with her when we were growing up. In time, each grandchild outgrew her. She was always happy and lived in the same space in time as a four- or five-year-old her entire life. After my Grandmother Eliser passed away, Tila started calling me, and my mother, Mommy. Tila kept me centered. It did not matter what kind of day I had at the office, when I would come home after a long day of work, Tila always greeted me with a big smile while she played with her dolls.

In Business – The Early Years

My father reopened his parent's restaurant and bar in 1966. I grew up working there, every day. My father expected us to think and perform like everyone else. The fact that we were young was irrelevant. My duties varied from paying bills to washing dishes. I remember one Saturday night when I first started managing other people. I was in the seventh grade, and my father had the two dishwashers report to me. They were older and cute, too. They ask me if they could leave early when we closed to go to the movies across the street. I said, "Sure." When my father came in and asked where they were, I told him, "I let them go early." He said,

"Fine. You will have to clean up alone." Though some of the other kitchen staff stayed that night, all they could do was keep me company. He didn't let anyone else help me, and I finished at 2 a.m. I never let them go early again.

Changes and Challenges

In 1977, my father had exploratory surgery and was diagnosed with cancer. My mother and I were the only ones there, because it was supposed to be exploratory surgery. I remember the doctor and the nun coming and asking us to join them in the chapel. His doctor then told us with tears in his eyes that my father only had two months to live. We brought him home because my mother wanted to take care of him at home. He died two months later to the day, on Mothers' Day. I was 14 and saw my mother age right before my eyes.

My father did not believe in life insurance, so when he died, we were wiped out financially. I remember paying his last medical bill 10 years later. My mother worked, I worked and went to high school, my grandmother helped out around the house, and my aunt played with her dolls. After my son was born, I worked and my mother and grandmother stayed home with my son and my aunt still played with her dolls. At this point, I had to figure out how to support our family of five without seriously changing our lifestyles again.

When my father died, the business was sold to settle his estate, and my mother was left with the receivables from the sale. I took the business back for my mother when the buyers defaulted on the loan from her. I then took over running the business, and I set out to sell it so I could do something else. I was not sure what, but I knew I did not want to run a restaurant. My hardest day in the technology industry is easier than any day in the food and beverage business. I knew we had to take it back because it was the best option, but it was not my preference. Since we could not afford an attorney, I did the paperwork without a lawyer. I asked questions and figured it out. I got everything back with the intention of selling it again but ended up running it for three more years.

Opening Night

I was 20 when the paperwork was finalized and the restaurant was once again ours, but we had to wait until my 21st birthday to reopen the business because I could not manage an establishment that sold liquor until I was 21. Opening night was memorable. I sat alone and counted the receipts and realized we had not made enough to break even. I was not sure how I was going to support my family. A couple of friends and I had done all the construction work ourselves and worked weeks, sometimes 24 hours a day, to renovate the place before opening.

It was months before we broke even. I cried every night; it was so hard. I came in early, worked lunch. I stayed at work between lunch and dinner. My mother would bring my son to stay with me at work and picked him up before dinner started. I closed the restaurant at 10 p.m. and the bar at 2 a.m. six days a week. On Sunday, I did payroll and other bookwork.

My First Computer

I decided to buy a computer to help run the business so I could spend more time with my son. The computer and accounting software were a huge investment at the time – about $8,000 in 1985. Like many new computer owners, I had questions and could not get technical support. I hired Ray Garcia, one of my brother's friends, to help me. He had just graduated from college with an accounting degree. He helped me set up the system and later became my company's first employee.

Talking about computers and accounting came easy for me, possibly because I had managed the books and taxes for the restaurant for so long. Soon, I was answering questions about the advantages of one general ledger package over another. Next, we began setting up systems for the local city government and a couple of other small businesses.

I finally sold the restaurant at the beginning of 1986 and was getting ready to go to college. Since it was between semesters, I looked for jobs and continued helping people buy computer systems. The job offers were never enough to support the household, though. One promising job was in Dallas. The company flew me out for an interview, but when I got there, I knew I could not move the whole family there. It was too far from home.

I saw greater opportunity in Albuquerque and expanded my consulting services there, despite the hour-and-a-half drive each way from Grants. My clientele grew quickly. Four months later, my son and I moved to Albuquerque, so I would not have to drive back and forth every day. I kept selling my time on installations and consultant services and then started selling whole systems to make sure everything was coordinated. Soon, I was handling the entire process. I made $125,000 my first year in this business.

McBride, Inc

McBride, Inc., is a business-to-business operation headquartered in Albuquerque. Our customers have a wide array of computing needs. We sell them computer hardware, software and professional technical service. We projected and exceeded $200 million in revenue with fewer than 500 employees in 1999. We look forward to tremendous growth, perhaps doubling in size over the next few years.

Although I felt comfortable with the decision to grow a business, I did not know that I was making a career choice when I started McBride and Associates. I knew I would do whatever it took to make it work. I had my family values and my experience, and I enjoyed the business.

The game of business is multifaceted, often complicated, sometimes surprisingly simple. To me, business consists of building value in a fair and dynamic way – for our associates and their families, our customers, our vendors and financiers.

Negotiating

From working with my father and my grandmother and having to make a living, I learned the art of negotiation. I had to negotiate hard when I was the main income generator for my whole family. I negotiated for everything from the purchase of a car to paying the plumber. I learned early on that I had to question and push a little or it would cost more. I also noticed that I would often be quoted one price but a man would be quoted another. I am not sure why this happens, but it does.

My job today, as then, is to ask questions. I negotiate on behalf of the company. I have always made the finance companies compete with each other. They tell me, for instance, that there are standards for loans to companies in my industry. I respond, "I need you and your organization to be our partner. I cannot survive in business over the long term if, for this amount of risk, you get this percentage of profit. Furthermore, you shouldn't be lending me money if I'm that irresponsible." They agree.

Customers

During the second quarter of 1999, Federal Computer, Inc., commissioned an independent industry survey of business customers. The survey had 88,000 respondents. Of seven total categories, McBride, Inc. ranked first in customer and product satisfaction. Two strengths stand out at McBride. First, we care about our customers. Second, we select projects on which we know we will be successful. Technology changes very quickly, and our success depends on staying ahead of the curve and matching what we can offer our customers with our infrastructure and its growth potential. This way, we assure our customers quality, success and longevity.

We look for long-term relationships. Our business partners expect us to make good business decisions. This ensures longevity for us and security for them. Why would they choose to do business with McBride in the future if they know they can push us to make poor business decisions? Being reasonable and responsible is an important part of making good business decisions. This requires that guidelines be fully understood and that information be accurate. Without these, when business people push – and most business people will – a CEO cannot know what or where the right decision should be.

Growth and Development

Even when the company was a one-person operation, I had a dynamic business plan. I knew how much I was going to make by the end of the year. Every year since then I have had a plan. During the year, our plan changes constantly. That is invigorating, but we always have a plan.

The second year I was in business, we more than doubled the revenue to $300,000. The third year we made $1.4 million, the next year $3 million. Then we went from $3 million to $8 million and $8 to $17 million. Our growth in 1998 was more than we did our entire eight years in business. We have experienced solid growth while building a foundation for future growth.

People often ask why McBride has grown so much so fast. I never planned to grow for growth's sake; the goal has always been to build a sustainable business that has value. Growth was the result of meeting our objectives for growth. As I thought about how to promote, manage and lead our growth, I knew it had to be balanced with development.

I make a distinction between growth and development. We are interested in sustainable long-term growth. To us, that means we concentrate on strategic development to achieve growth. We deliberately develop the organizational process and systems or infrastructure that position us to meet our future growth objectives.

We plan our growth and make sure we have the infrastructure to support it. There were only two years when we did not have the infrastructure to support significant growth. We were at the maximum capacity of our computer system. That year we knew we could not grow much, but we still grew by about $5 million.

In a year's time we invested and installed a new computer system. That same year, we also changed the organization: specifically, the main processes that supported our customers and sales. We did a quality analysis of everything and streamlined processes. It was a team effort. The entire organization, under the leadership of our chief financial officer, John Irick, and a dedicated team of 20 people, worked through the technical and process changes without missing a beat. As far as our customers were concerned, the service just kept getting better.

Financing Growth

I did not use any proceeds from the restaurant when I started McBride. The restaurant belonged to my mother. She was in her early 50s and had many good years ahead of her. In the beginning, my customers paid me up-front – that is how I initially funded the company. As I grew, my customers paid 50 percent down with their orders. Then I eventually went to a 30-day billing cycle.

When I added the computer hardware side of the business, my banker, Tony Esparza, gave us a line of credit against my receivables. Initially, I had a $10,000 line of credit. Soon we grew to the bank's maximum lending limit of $250,000. At that point, I researched our options and selected a finance company.

Finance companies have no lending limits because they are not part of the Federal Reserve System guarantee, they use their own money and are responsible for their own losses. We started out with a $2 million line. Then it grew to $5 million, then $10 million. Today we have over $60 million dollars in credit to draw from.

Developing a Company Culture

In my opinion, treating people with respect is not a choice; it is a way of life. I learned this from my family, especially my parents and grandparents. They treated all people with respect. Age, race, religion, sex, abilities, wealth – differences did not matter, everyone was treated with respect.

Though I learned early on that not everyone had these values, I also learned early that these values could contribute to the success of a business. People respond differently to the same situation. Predicting a person's response is a gamble I choose not to take. Most people deserve a chance. Some people recognize the learning opportunity and become highly valuable to the organization. Others do not.

Those who abuse the system eventually must leave. We have a responsibility to everybody in the company, as well as to our customers, vendors and partners, to make sure we have the best people on the job.

Sometimes, after the fact, we recognize we should have done something earlier; but we cannot act prematurely, because I feel everyone deserves a chance. You never know who will recognize the principle, embrace it and grow from the experience.

Attracting the Best People

We attract the best people in this industry, which makes our organization very diverse. At the end of a recent interview I asked, "Why would you want to join our company?" The person said, "Knowing what I know about your company, I feel I would have greater potential and opportunities at your company than where I am today." To me that meant, "Given my age and race, your organization affords me the highest opportunities."

We did not set out to have a diverse worforce; we set out to hire the best people for the job. I believe most people can sense immediately whether they are accepted or not. It is not surprising that during an interview, those senses are heightened and people know whether their obvious differences of race, age, color or sex are accepted or not.

It is difficult to present yourself in the best light if you feel a lack of acceptance. If, when you walk in, you realize the interviewer does not notice or care about your age or whether you are a man or a woman, or what color your skin is or anything else, it does not get in your way. You feel comfortable presenting the best that you are.

The leadership at McBride might jokingly say I beat acceptance and tolerance into them; and, in a sense, they are right. Associates know they are not going to get away with discrimination. They cannot stay at McBride if they do not understand this. I have no tolerance for sexism, racism or any other "ism," absolutely none. You would be escorted to the door the day we concluded an investigation and found grounds for such a complaint.

Associates Lead

Turnover is an important part of the development of any organization – if not managed, turnover can be costly for any company. This is especially true in our industry, where technological change requires a tremendous, ongoing investment in training. We have lower turnover than the industry average by about half, but we do have turnover. Most of our turnover is in entry-level positions and should happen within the first 90 days of employment.

I feel that every associate is important. I enjoy the people in the business more than anything. We provide an environment where our associates understand that every position in the company is important. Each person has the opportunity to contribute to the overall plan. Because we often promote from within and are, in essence, hiring our future leaders, we have developed a hiring and training process that requires the commitment of every person within the organization.

People lead themselves. Leadership is about each person taking responsibility for his or her actions and for the growth of the company. My leadership role in the company is to advise the rest of the leaders. However, most important for me is receiving advice from the leaders of our company. My role is to set strategy and vision for the company as a whole, and to create value for the associates, the organization, our customers and the communities we serve.

I cannot lead people to do their jobs. I think people have to lead themselves, and they have to make a commitment to do the things they choose to do. We try to identify individuals who have leadership characteristics. Everyone we hire should have the potential to become a strong leader someday, and every area of the company must have people with great potential.

The Future of McBride

The future looks good for McBride, Inc. The market is changing, and we are changing along with it. We provide a set of solutions to a market where the need for technology solutions grows every day. It is vital that as we grow, we maintain a secure foundation for that growth. Our growth will come from internal organic development and from acquisitions. We just completed our first acquisition: a division of GEC, Inc., called Marconi Information Systems, Inc.

It looks like McBride, Inc. is ready to continue its aggressive growth, but I believe that when all is said and done, the most important part of our foundation is growing an organization where the associates on our team feel that we are making a difference.

Managing Communication

Communication is essential in all companies. In our ever-changing industry, it is vital. We have always conducted monthly and annual all-staff meetings.

We call the monthly meeting "A Journey to Excellence." The purpose is to share the vision and to make sure everybody is working with the same agenda. It is not just a matter of buying into a vision; it is a matter of fully understanding it and its implications. We discuss the status of the company and the long-term perspectives. For instance, in a recent meeting we discussed our acquisition strategy. We might also discuss new business practices. I would say 95 percent of the associates attend. If they cannot attend in person, they hook up by telephone.

Our annual meeting is a part of our technology and industry training week. We discuss our performance data, our strategic plan, our annual goals and customer information on the first day. The rest of the week is dedicated to training the staff on technology and technical practices.

I have stayed up many nights reviewing budgets, first at the restaurant and now for McBride, Inc. The financial data are the pulse of the organization. I rely on the numbers and analyze the results from each division to understand the health of the organization and how much value we have added at any given point. Managers are responsible for explaining why a number is off the projections. I manage conservatively, because that is my personal comfort level.

Committing to Lifelong Learning

Education is a lifelong pursuit. School ends, degrees are granted, but an individual's education never stops. Entrepreneurs tend to take this to heart by constantly seeking ways to improve their business and their leadership skills. I learned from my family that to learn, you must first realize you do not have all the answers. They taught me that to receive new information, I had to admit I did not know everything. Each of us as individuals has the ability to learn continuously.

When I was starting out, I knew I was in an industry that had tremendous potential. To figure out my potential, I looked at big companies, even companies that were in a different industry. I studied them on a regular basis.

I also looked at our competitors and studied how they were doing things. Many competitors from our early years are no longer in business. I analyzed what went wrong so I would not make the same mistakes. I read the books written by the founders and the people who helped them grow. I studied their principles and strategies.

Getting information about companies was most difficult during my first years in business. I wanted to know what made a company successful, how it handled growth and the many challenges that businesses overcome.

I was benchmarking. I was comparing their infrastructure, processes and ratios with ours. Today, I am able to compare McBride and Associates with publicly held companies. I look for the same information to see where we are tracking.

Giving Back to the Community

My father gave to his community, never expecting anything in return. To him, it was a responsibility. I give to my community for many reasons. One is to honor family members who are no longer with us; another is to respond to need. There are intelligent children in our communities who need support, guidance and mentoring.

The success at McBride, Inc. has allowed me to establish the McBride Foundation. Our flagship program is called College Bound. We established this program to create a national awareness that "children are the future of our society and our world." As a society, we say that children are our future. However, treatment of our children suggests otherwise.

Life is precious, and each of us has the opportunity to enhance life each day. Through College Bound, children create a personal foundation that will help them enhance their own lives. The objective of the program is to reduce the dropout and crime rates among our youth. The program inspires the participants to finish high school and pursue higher education.

If we do not help them develop, they are going to grow up waiting for someone to do something for them, instead of doing it for themselves. I hope this program will add value to the lives of all participants, especially the children.

Being a Woman Entrepreneur

Early on, people would ask me, "Isn't it hard being a woman entrepreneur?" I always said, "No." I did not want them to feel sorry for me by letting them know that it was in fact very hard. Unfortunately, we live in a world where people judge others based on external elements. I feel that the entire world loses when our minds are closed.

You can look anywhere from a day-care center to a home for the elderly and find that we pre-judge people without even knowing them, based on what people look like and sound like. When I meet people who are uncomfortable with female executives, I have to change their mind or move on. I often choose to move on. My father used to tell me, "You can't change the world, just yourself."

As a businessperson, I add value by keeping my focus on the business. We have a better solution, we have better customer service and we have the infrastructure to support continued growth. We will be around for our customers for a long time. We have an experienced and talented staff, working for an organization that appreciates their differences and their contributions.

I believe I ultimately gain the trust of businesspeople, if not their respect, despite what they might feel about doing business with a woman. At the end of the day, they do business with us because we have a better solution.

Epilogue – Keeping Perspective

Growing up, I heard my father say, "It is important to keep perspective." I started and built a business with the purpose of making a difference in the world. One of my joys in life is watching things grow – everything from flowers to people, myself and associates included. I have a deep admiration and appreciation for the people who work at McBride. Many have been with me for a long time, and we have all grown as the company has grown.

We also have noticed that our families have grown and prospered. I have always thought it is not just about the individuals that show up every day, it is about their families. We do not just hire the individual; we hire the entire family. My intention was to build the company's foundation to support all its families. We keep this perspective and our commitments. Our associates made McBride what it is today, and they are our future.

CHAPTER EIGHT

Carlos A. Saladrigas
A Personnel Pioneer

THE VINCAM GROUP INC.
MIAMI, FLORIDA

Industry: Professional Employee Services

Date Started: November 12, 1992

Revenue: $1.44 Billion

Rate of Growth 1998-1999: 25%

Awards, Board Memberships and Accomplishments:

2000 Trustee, University of Miami

2000 Member of the Board, Belen Jesuit
Preparatory School and St. Thomas University

2000 Co-Chair, The Miami-Dade Alliance
for Ethical Government

1998 Champions of Higher Independent Education
in Florida Awarded to Carlos and Olga Maria Saladrigas

1998 Hispanic Business 500, Largest Hispanic Business

My mother, Elisa Landaluce de Saladrigas, was an entrepreneur and businesswoman in Cuba. She kept a positive outlook on life, and I inherited that trait from her.

She operated a very chic clothing store in Havana and was ahead of her time in her marketing and customer service strategies. For instance, she held fashion shows and did personalized shopping, things that were rarely done anywhere else at this time.

Unfortunately, she opened her store as Castro was heating up his revolution. Two years before he took over, bomb threats and murders in Havana's streets kept people at home. The bad soon turned ugly, and my mother had to close the store.

My parents feared for my future in Cuba and in 1961, when I was just 12, they took desperate measures to get me off the island through a plan called Operation Peter Pan (*Operación Pedro Pan*), the second-largest underground railroad in modern history.

Significant controversy surrounds Operation Peter Pan, and rumors of both abuse and heroism abound; but it brought about 14,000 children to the United States during a five-year period.[1] Most of the children, like me, came to live with relatives, but others were placed in orphanages and government institutions.[2]

The hardest part of being in the United States was moving from family to family the year before my parents joined me. Those were hard times for Cuban immigrant families. It was difficult feeding an extra person, so I was never able to stay with any one family for long.

Now, as the father of four children, I can appreciate the heartache my parents must have felt to see me leave. I am sure it was tougher on them than it was on me. Despite the constant change in households, I managed to deliver newspapers, mow lawns and wash and wax cars to earn money. It was tough, but I worked hard and saved every cent I could.

When my parents joined me a year later, the $400 I had saved allowed us to get started in our new life.

My English was so poor that I failed the eighth grade. After I reunited with my parents, they secured a scholarship for me to attend Belén Jesuit Preparatory School in downtown Miami. This school had been founded in Cuba over 100 years earlier. When Castro seized and nationalized the schools, the priests fled to Miami and reopened the school there. Today it is the only school in the United States that can boast more than 150 years of uninterrupted history in two countries. I completed ninth and tenth grades there. Those two years were happy ones for me.

When I was in the 10th grade, my mother developed throat cancer. It progressed rapidly and, by the time I was in the 11th grade, she could no longer work. I had to drop out of school and get a job to help with the household and medical expenses.

My first full-time job was as an office boy with a company called Arvida Corp., a large real estate developer in Miami. I supplemented my income by selling just about everything that would fit on my moped. I sold purses, hanging three or four on each handlebar. I also sold shoes that I ordered by mail. Usually, I sold door to door.

During that time I met Olga, my future wife. We both were teaching catechism at St. John Bosco Church in Miami, and I saw her as a potential customer. Before I realized I was attracted to her, I tried to sell her a pair of shoes.

I made about $3.50 on each pair of shoes I sold and had to pay $1.50 in postage for every pair I returned. Unfortunately, none of the shoes I brought her fit quite right, so I had to send them back. This wreaked havoc on my cash flow and, ultimately, on the bottom line. Soon, I realized I was in the hole. I asked her if she would forget about buying shoes and buy a set of Encyclopedia Britannica instead. She wasn't interested in that, but we ended up dating and became engaged. I had just turned 18 and she was 16.

Soon after that, my mother passed away. Nine months later, in August 1968, Olga and I got married. I was 19 and she was 17. To this day, we are not sure why her parents did not object to our marriage. We certainly would have objected if one of our children had wanted to marry so young.

Olga and I sometimes talk about those days. Olga had left Cuba in 1965 at age 15. Before leaving, she experienced tremendous hardships that I did not have to endure because I had left earlier. The years from 1961 to 1965 in Cuba were years of persecution and constant anxiety when people always wondered when the proverbial knock on the door in the middle of the night would come.

The young people who left Cuba in the early years, especially those who lived under the Castro regime, never had the luxury of being teenagers. Those experiences propelled us into early adulthood, skipping our adolescence altogether. Olga and I have concluded that our commitment of a lifetime was a natural choice for us. Her parents must have understood.

I finished high school by taking night classes and graduated 10 days before our wedding. Ten days after our wedding, I started classes at Miami Dade Community College. I wanted to complete school as fast as I could. Each semester I took the maximum number of evening hours allowed. I carried a 15-semester-hour schedule and held a full-time job. I attended two classes every night, Monday through Thursday, and classes all day Saturday. I do not know how I was able to carry that kind of load. It was rough going, but I somehow had the energy to do it.

As soon as I completed as many credits as I needed at Miami Dade, I transferred to the University of Miami, where I continued taking a full load at night. I skipped vacations and went to school year-round. This allowed me to get my bachelor's degree in accounting in 1971, after three years, graduating in the top 2 percent of my class.

We had our first baby, our daughter Elisa, a year after we were married. Olga was still in high school during her pregnancy and had to attend adult classes instead of the local high school. That was the policy in those days.

During that time, something extremely important happened to me. One of my bosses at Arvida, Charlie Dean, did what I think every human being should do for another: He became my mentor and advocate. At first, he casually suggested that I go to graduate school and get an MBA. With every excuse I made for not going, he painted an even bigger vision for me.

His dream was not just that I get an MBA, but that I get an MBA at a top school, such as Harvard, Stanford, Wharton or Chicago. I said, "Charlie, you're crazy. What is a Cuban going to do there? I don't have any money. I have a wife and a child and I owe a lot of money to the University of Miami."

I was desperate to work, but Charlie told me not to worry, to just apply to schools and let the rest follow. He was so insistent and I was so resistant that he actually wrote to each school and got application packages for me. He then paid the application fees after I told him I could not afford them. He literally forced me to apply.

To my surprise, Harvard accepted me to its MBA program on a deferred admission. I was guaranteed admission after two years' more substantive work experience. I put Harvard in the back of my mind, thinking it was two years away. In 1971, I took a job with Arthur Young & Co., an accounting firm in Jacksonville, Florida. My first son, Carlos Jr., was born there in 1972.

The life of a first-year accountant in a major accounting firm is tough. They really put me through the grinder. Despite the job, we still had to supplement our income. I taught accounting at the local college in the evenings and did bookkeeping for a few small businesses on the side. Those two years were good years. We had a good life. Our apartment was small, but it was nice. Then came the time to act on the deferred admission. Time had flown, and we decided I would go to Harvard. Charlie was right. Things worked out.

I left Arthur Young in 1973 and headed for Boston in a rented truck, towing our little car behind us. I was once again a student. Fortunately, I had a substantial scholarship and other assistance to help me pay for school and living expenses. We were now a family of four, so we rented an apartment off campus.

To make ends meet I taught accounting again, this time at Bentley College in Waltham, Massachusetts. Our second son, Luis, was born in February 1975, during my second year at Harvard. I graduated in June with second-year honors.

Soon after graduation I got a job with Peat, Marwick and Mitchell in Miami, and we moved back in the summer of 1975. I worked there for about two years and then went on to a job with PepsiCo. It was a fantastic job. Congress had just enacted the Foreign Corrupt Practices Act, and all the multinational companies were concerned about the control of their branches in Latin America.

PepsiCo asked me to set up an office anywhere I wanted – in Latin America, New York or Miami – and to hire a staff. Our new office was to be responsible for auditing PepsiCo's Latin American businesses. I proceeded to hire a number of colleagues from Peat, Marwick and Mitchell, including José (Pepe) Sánchez, my current partner at Vincam. Our new office was near my home.

Travel was an important part of the job, and my colleagues and I always traveled together. We were friends; we got along well and had some great times. We must have done a good job because within two years, everyone in the group was promoted to another important position within PepsiCo. I was promoted to the head of corporate and strategic planning, where I worked with top-level management. It was a high-pressure, high-profile, fast-track kind of job, but very interesting. It would have taken me years, otherwise, to work myself up to these levels.

With this promotion came another move for my family. I was transferred to PepsiCo headquarters in Purchase, New York, and we moved to Ridgefield, Connecticut. We spent less than two years there, and then I was asked to go to Mexico City.

Just as I accepted that job, I learned that Olga was pregnant with our third son, Jorge. That complicated our lives, because we thought it would be better for her to stay in the States during her pregnancy. I started my job in Mexico City in January 1981, and for the next six months I commuted every week between Mexico City and New York City. I left New York on Monday mornings and came back on Friday afternoons.

In June, when the children were out of school, we returned to our house in Miami. Jorge was born that August, and soon afterward we moved to Mexico City. The next four-and-a-half years were great for us. We learned to experience and enjoy Latin culture as a family. Despite its size and pollution problems, Mexico City still afforded a comfortable lifestyle. We were all happy.

The professional side of life was a completely different story, however. The economy of Mexico went through major changes, ranging from monetary devaluation to inflation to stagnation and to nationalization of the banking system.

By coincidence, my good friend Pepe Sánchez, who also had been moving around within PepsiCo, was assigned to the Mexico City office. After two years, we were once again working together. By 1984, the pollution, the traffic and the thought of moving several more times as part of my job caused Olga and me to seriously consider leaving PepsiCo.

We simply did not cherish the thought of moving, especially when it could be to anywhere on the globe. Our children were growing up, and we felt they needed the stability of roots. We moved back to our house in Miami.

Shortly after our return to Miami, Pepe joined us. I had been entertaining the idea of starting my own company, and he also had considered starting a business. As expatriate employees, he and I each had accumulated some extra capital, so we began searching for opportunities. We came up with a number of ideas. We started a gourmet pizza parlor that we thought had an interesting concept – over 33 different toppings, ranging from exotic pineapple and ham to shrimp to guava and cheese. The restaurant did not do well, and we were not really satisfied with this venture.

One Saturday morning, while waiting for Pepe at my house, I picked up a business magazine and read about a company in Texas that was outsourcing human resources. The idea caught my attention. Over breakfast, I started sketching my idea on a napkin and continued it on writing paper.

That Texas company went out of business soon after that, but we did not give their misfortune a second thought. The idea of outsourcing human resources quickly took form as our business plan. Despite our optimism, we still wanted a second opinion – or perhaps confirmation that this was not just a good plan but also a great opportunity.

We submitted our plan to our colleagues and friends at Peat, Marwick and Mitchell for review. A couple of weeks later, they gave us a 16-page memo in which they outlined the difficulties of starting and growing such a business. Their final recommendation was that we not get into it. But we had considered all the risks and arrived at the opposite conclusion. Our optimism propelled us to move quickly. By the time we received the memo, we were already in business. It was too late to change course.

In question were the issues of fundamental operations. Labor laws and regulations are a central part of this business. With labor and employment activities come the Internal Revenue code and associated regulations. Our advisers had concluded that the industry was overly regulated and that would offset the market need. We, on the other hand, were convinced that in this case logic would prevail over bureaucracy.

The Economies, Our Fundamental Pillars

We could not ignore that 16-page memo because we trusted the source. We also trusted our business plan, especially its long-term prospects. The service made sense, it was real and it was needed. Whenever you have an opportunity where your market or your potential market is structurally inefficient and you have an opportunity to rationalize those inefficiencies, you have a business. We believed those things were in place, so it was easy to fuel our continued optimism.

We understood this business well. The state of the industry, the regulations and the novelty of the business concept added up to a difficult beginning. Eventually, we created four very fundamental economies that small businesses, our customers, did not have.

This was our opportunity. We wanted to provide a complete outsourcing solution that reduced the risks of managing human resources. That, along with a dedicated sales staff, became our overall business strategy.

Risk, from employee practices, health care and worker's compensation benefits, is the part of human resources that most small business owners do not handle efficiently. But while risk is a burden for the small business owner, it was an opportunity for us. We counted on four economies – scale, scope, distribution and focus – to address the risk issue squarely.

These economies allowed us to provide human resources benefits and services that assisted business owners in attracting and retaining high-caliber employees while focusing on their core business. This, in turn, improved the lives of the co-leased employees and allowed us to create jobs and provide an enriched work environment for our internal staff. This was a business proposition that benefited all parties.

Economy of Scale

When you have 50,000 employees, you can buy things and do things that small employers cannot. When we were very small, we really did not have an intrinsic advantage over our clients. In fact, we had some clients who were larger than we were. Today we can offer small businesses fringe benefit packages equivalent to or even better than those offered by Fortune 500 employers.

It is common for new employees to get better benefits. We can make that part of the process much easier for business owners, whose success depends on the quality of their employees. They can attract highly qualified employees looking for competitive benefits packages.

When you deal with risk, it is not effective to simply aggregate it, because when you aggregate bad risk you end up with a huge bad risk. Therefore, economies of scale alone did not make a business opportunity for us.

Economy of Scope

We also created economies of scope. We can provide a wide range of services. Economies of scope allowed us to do more things to better and more effectively manage large aggregated risks.

We now have the volume and can do things to control risk that were never possible at client work sites before. This creates additional efficiencies. For instance, we are able to implement safety programs at our clients' locations that are generally out of the question for companies of that size. It also allows us to protect some employees when a layoff becomes necessary. Laid-off workers from one company might be placed at another client's business.

Economy of Distribution

The third economy that we created is the economy of distribution. When clients outsource their human resources to us, we probably do the things that would take 10 or 15 individual suppliers to provide, ranging from payroll to risk management to worker's compensation. We bundle all of that into one sale, so we create an enormous economy of distribution for our customers. This is one-stop shopping for business owners.

Signing on new clients covers the cost of their acquisition. Providing additional specialized services adds profit without additional costs. We can provide products and services beyond those that other professional employer organizations (PEOs) currently deliver. That is how our growth and operations models work together to make us highly competitive.

Economy of Focus

The last economy we create for our customers is the economy of focus. Managing the cost of human resources is our only business. For our clients it is, at best, a marginal activity. We devote more attention to the quality of services to employees and to the business owners than the owners could themselves. We have lawyers on staff to interpret the law for our customers. Vincam spends $5 million a year on technology and shares information with its clients. We employ a physician and 40 nurses who provide training in health and safety procedures to small business staffs. This includes heavy equipment safety and drug testing for all employees. Safety records of PEO employees have improved because of our focus on safety.

When we put these four economies together, we were convinced we had a business that would succeed. I knew there were many obstacles out there – regulatory, governmental

and legislative. Nevertheless, when I looked at the fundamentals, I said, "This is a real business opportunity." That
conviction fueled the optimism that allowed us to stay in
business when others were questioning the practicality of
our ideas.

The Early Years and Today

The idea of outsourcing human resources has evolved
tremendously since we started Vincam. The beginning was
difficult. It was very hard to say to a client, "We can do it better." The benefit to the employer then was convenience and
quality. As a new industry with lagging government regulations, we were not sure how much "better" we were than
internal human resources functions. Today I don't hesitate to
say we can do it better, because we now have an internal staff
of 650 to do it, experts in just about every conceivable area of
human resources. When we were small we could not say
that, so it was a difficult proposition.

Interestingly and fortunately for us, we found that small-
to medium-sized entrepreneurial firms were happy to get rid
of the headache that comes with payroll, worker's compensation and other government compliance activities. In their
eyes, we were a better option even if we did not represent
bottom-line savings.

Today we offer a comprehensive human resources service
similar to that of a large corporation. Perhaps the most significant outcome of our growth for our clients is our capacity to provide a customized human resources experience, not
just its functions.

A good internal human resources function contributes to
that intangible culture that defines an organization. It is
much more than government compliance, guarding against
lawsuits and the technicalities of compensation and benefits.
Human resources services envelop operations and give an

organization its distinct flavor. At the employee level, human resources is the area that guards employee rights, helps maintain a safe environment and rewards employee performance.

Now, in partnership with entrepreneurs, we can affect the growth of organizational cultures that support operational growth while minimizing risk. Customizing services means attending to those details that affect performance. If a client needs a human resources director on site, we can provide that. If employees at a work site need next-day counseling and support because a co-worker died in a car accident, we can provide that. Or if an employee threatens a lawsuit, we can provide the business owner an immediate, objective opinion about options.

Training and management development are two areas of human resources that baffle both new business owners and corporate giants. They can be expensive, the quality of training programs is uncertain, and sometimes they conflict with internal processes. We now have Vincam University, which offers employee training and management development for our clients on such topics as customer service, management skills and organizational development.

Quality control for training is as important as quality control for the more technical aspects of human resources. The client can count on consistent quality and a single source for training and development services. Today we can say that our clients get bottom-line savings with increased benefits to the business owner and the employees.

Years One and Two

That 16-page memo made many valuable points. It took nine months after opening our doors before we had our first client. It was frustrating, but we managed in spite of it. I worked for an HMO to support my family. My partner, Pepe,

worked full-time in our business. Since he did not have children, his monthly expenses were much lower than mine, so
he could afford to go longer without a salary.

At the HMO I learned about the health-care business. That
experience reinforced my conviction that our business would
succeed. I saw how difficult it was for a small business to
manage the complex processes of compensation and employee benefits. With that in mind, we just stuck with it and, little by little, our business began to work.

We had founded our company in 1984. In March of 1986
I left my job at the HMO. It was a family business, owned by
two brothers. They had a big fight and I was one of the
casualties. By that September things went from bad to worse.
I had just enough in my bank account to make the October
mortgage payment. Things looked pretty dismal, and I
thought I would have to abandon our PEO business and find
another job.

Luckily, a good friend of mine who was an administrator
at a local hospital got me a consulting engagement. The
hospital was interested in setting up a physician-hospital
organization, a PHO. I had acquired significant knowledge
about health care by then. The consulting engagement
amounted to $8,000 a month. If it had not been for that, Pepe
and I probably would not be in business today.

Self-Discipline and a Fundamental Strategy

With that break, I could again concentrate my efforts on
the business. We continued to grow slowly. We reinvested
almost everything into the business, and we disciplined
ourselves to take very little money out of it. We were careful
not to mix personal and business expenses and activities.
We kept everything clean because it reflected our personal
style and because by then, our industry had developed a
formidable black eye.

Getting into the PEO industry was easy. The cash flow was good, there was a long time between actions and consequences, and regulatory oversight was minimal despite a tremendous number of outdated regulations. This was a ready recipe for fraudulent behavior. In fact, several cases of fraud in the industry made prominent headlines during those years. This gave regulators a further incentive to try to crush us. We chose to prove ourselves by our example.

Pepe and I both are accountants. We are not human resources professionals. We capitalized on our strengths, experiences and skills. We knew how to get to the systems internally, not only the computer systems, but the entire organization of systems. We banked on our experience in understanding work flow and how to create efficiencies. We probably can attribute some of our skills and a great degree of our success to our strong orientation to strategic planning.

The experience at PepsiCo had been invaluable. We are particularly good at identifying market opportunities and understanding what kinds of strategies we need to develop to be successful in those markets. We spent a lot of time and resources doing strategic analysis and fine-tuning our strategies. We stuck to our strengths in a field in which we initially had no expertise.

We built the business on one fundamental strategy: the belief that, particularly in service businesses, people-based competitive advantages are much more enduring than technology-based competitive advantages. Although we always invest in technological advantages, those are short-lived and constantly changing. Competitors can emulate them, given enough time.

But when you build your competitive advantages around people – and that implies creating a supportive culture with training and development – they endure. This concept is easy to understand and difficult to emulate. Clearly, our biggest competitive advantage is the spirit of our people and the level of service that we have created as part of the culture at Vincam.

We like to say that we sell time, knowledge and care. Generally, clients like to hear one song, one they recognize and appreciate. Writing the musical score might be the role of the CEO, but the rest is up to the employees. Vincam is like a symphony orchestra. Everybody's music plays a part in it. If even one person is out of tune, the piece does not sound right. We have found that everyone needs to understand clearly how each fits into the overall context of the service we deliver to our clients.

Our culture supports our employees so that the client comes first. To the client, this means we are totally accessible. We grew the company in the belief that there should not be more than three levels between the CEO and the client. That kind of commitment and that kind of accessibility are important. Our people are devoted to client service. Whether it is their particular job or not, they take care of the client. Every one of my clients has my beeper number, but none ever calls me. They don't need to. Our clients know they can reach me. They can reach anybody at Vincam.

Helping to Create an Industry

The regulatory situation presented us with an interesting option, which we readily accepted. We had to recreate the industry or be put out of business. We became a founding member of what was then called the National Staff Leasing Association, now the National Association of Professional Employer Organizations (NAPEO). This soon became the industry's trade association.

I was elected president of the association. Part of my responsibility was to lobby on behalf of the association to organizations like the National Council for Compensation Insurance (NCCI), state unemployment commissioners and the U.S. Department of Labor. I lobbied state legislatures and regulators all the way from Maine to Oregon.

We did not have offices in any of those states, but we knew that until we had an industry that was accepted and valued, our individual businesses would not succeed. We spent a significant amount of time and resources – I probably spent as much as half of my time – creating and building the industry. It was an incredibly long shot. In fact, most people today tell me they never thought we would succeed.

Florida was the first state to pass industry-specific licensing regulations. I wrote the bill for that, lobbying actively before the legislature. The bill was passed in 1991. It gave us legitimacy as an industry. Right after that, the industry began to grow rapidly.

Expanding Outside of Florida

The year 1991 was a watershed for us. We had grown substantially by then. We had 20 to 30 internal employees and, in our first venture outside Florida, decided to open an operation in Michigan. We had been advised that getting a stronger foothold in Florida was a better option than expanding outside the state. Why take the risk when we had growth opportunities in Florida? But we knew we had to prove that we could operate as a business outside of our back yard, so we entered into a partnership in Detroit.

By 1992, when Hurricane Andrew hit, our company was solid and the hurricane had little effect our business. We did not miss any of our payrolls. Expansion had paid off.

Vincam's Growth and the IPO

We knew the market and we knew its size. Our customers are businesses that employ as few as 10 and as many as 1,000 people. We have clients at both ends of the spectrum. Our target customers are companies that have somewhere between 10 and 500 employees. These companies are among the fastest growing in the United States.

Job creation over the last 10 to15 years has happened mostly in the small business sector because the larger employers have been downsizing and outsourcing functions. More than half of all employed Americans work for small businesses. Such a market has a potential revenue over $1 trillion.

The PEO industry has less than 3 percent penetration of the total potential market. In real numbers that means that by the year 2007, professional employer organizations will employ 37 million people, up from 2.5 million in 1995. Even today, the market potential is enormous, and the market keeps growing as new businesses start and grow in record numbers.

In 1993 we continued to grow and had to move. Our new home was a four-story, 22,000-square-foot building, which was a lot of added space for us at the time. We continued growing and we have built a new headquarters, which was finished in early 1999. It has about 95,000 square feet and is close to our original site.

Today, 650 internal staff members support another 50,000 external employees nationwide. We have offices in Miami, Ft. Lauderdale, West Palm Beach and Orlando, Florida; Atlanta; Manchester, New Hampshire; Orange, Connecticut; Rochester, New York; two offices in Detroit; Grand Rapids, Michigan; Green Bay, Wisconsin; Denver; Los Angeles; and El Paso, Texas.

This was not an overnight success. It took years for that initial plan to become a fast-growing business. We have well over $1 billion in revenues. We are actually growing faster than the industry standard of 20 percent a year. Historically, we have grown at 50 percent. Our target is to continue to grow the business about 30 percent annually.

By the time the outsourcing trend began, we were an experienced firm. Being on the forefront of that wave has been beneficial to us. Today outsourcing is common practice and we feel it has not reached its maturity, especially considering the potential market in telecommuting and home-based businesses. These areas are likely to be regulatory headaches and potential growth markets for us.

We were in a business where we had to grow. We wanted to make some strategic acquisitions. The industry was very fragmented, and acquisitions were and still are a great opportunity. Up to a certain point we had financed our own growth, but after that we required substantial capital. It is easier to grow when you have publicly traded stock, which gives you a great currency to effect acquisitions.

Going public is a tough decision. You must ask yourself, "Is this the right year? Am I ready for it? Is the company ready for this change? Do we have the right controls and the right kind of visibility of earning for the next few quarters to make sure we are making the right move?"

The key areas are management, know-how, internal accounting controls, financial reporting and the ability to predict the future with a fairly high degree of accuracy. It is a bold and risky decision. Nevertheless, we went ahead, and it turned out to be a very good decision.

We took the company public in May 1996. It was a very successful IPO for us and for our investors. We have met analysts' expectations every quarter since then. Going public allowed us to continue to grow the business. We have more than doubled the size of the company since we did so.

Going public also had a noticeable internal effect. All of a sudden, I began hearing comments from among our people everywhere: "We have arrived." "This is a major step forward." "This is a big business now." "We are really in the big leagues." It served as an energizer for our organization. Overall, it was an exciting step.

Community Service

Growing as fast as we did and realizing the potential of that initial business plan placed a special responsibility upon us. My Jesuit education had given me a clear purpose in life. The priests taught us that we have a special duty to maximize the gifts and skills we have received – whatever they may be – and do the best we can. It is our responsibility to work as hard as we can for the betterment of the world around us. That has always been my guiding light.

I chose to use my gifts and do my best in the area of commerce and business. We have created a great number of jobs where none existed before. We created wealth in the community. We have gathered a group of people to work together in a cohesive and honest way, based on our set of values. We want everyone at Vincam to feel good about what each brings to the company, and we consider each person a major contributor.

We also have provided a high level of service to our clients by managing their human resources in a fair, equitable and legal way. Together we have made our society and our community a better place. That is very satisfying to me. It is a big part of what I need to do, and I take this responsibility very seriously.

Ethics in Government

Because I believe strongly in supporting our communities' growth potential, I serve on several boards. Two organizations have touched me personally. I am on the board of the Belén Jesuit Preparatory School of Miami, where my children and I attended school. Recently, I chaired the Juvenile Diabetes Foundation Walk. I was first prompted to support this when we almost lost our youngest son, Jorge, to diabetes.

Also important to me is the issue of corporate, business and governmental ethics. Last year I became involved in *La Mesa Redonda* (The Round Table), and launched an effort against official corruption. This organization has been very successful. It has galvanized the whole community to work in the fight against corruption.

La Mesa Redonda comprises 30 prominent Hispanic enterprise leaders who meet monthly to discuss issues relevant to our local community and to the Hispanic community in particular. As individuals, we are interested in determining what we can do to influence positive change in our communities. It is a great group – active, dynamic and caring.

As headlines about corruption in Miami increased, we worried about the implications for us as a community. From the business perspective, ethics is the underpinning of a solid economy and a requirement for a stable democracy. If Miami is perceived as being increasingly corrupt, it will seriously affect our community.

Miami is our home. Our children live here, and we cannot afford to see our community go down the path of corruption. A reasonable trust in government is important to the well-being of communities. If corruption persists, companies may decide to invest or locate in other cities. Taxpayers may vote for reductions in spending at a time when we need new roads and an airport to handle our growth. Tourists may decide on other, safer, family-oriented destinations.

To try to turn things around, we called for a one-day summit of 50 community leaders from different sectors: corporate, community, religious, education and government. Three themes evolved. One, that business cannot be unethical or amoral. Pursuing profit is not synonymous with unethical behavior. Two, as entrepreneurs and business owners we are responsible for making sure ethics and morality are part of the way we do business. Three, as businesspeople we have to take a leading role in cleaning out corruption in Dade County. At the end of the day, when it comes to governmental corruption, it takes two to tango. The summit was extremely successful.

From this summit grew another organization, the Miami-Dade Alliance for Ethical Government (M-DAEG). This new organization has 125 trustees, a board of directors and an executive committee. Gerald Hogan, retired chief justice of the Supreme Court of Florida, is the president. We hope that in three years we will have effected changes in procurement practices, lobbying and the entire election process, including election financing, term limits and the compensation of public officials

As an example of how corruption in high places can affect perceptions, I was alarmed to learn that after Hurricane Mitch, people hesitated to send aid to Hondurans and Guatemala because they were not sure whether the aid would reach the people that needed it. That is the ultimate effect of perceived or actual corruption. We cannot afford to sit back and idly watch our community follow this road.

Ethics in Business

Ethics is essential to business operations. Every decision has an ethical impact. Without a culture that stresses ethics, it is easy to cut corners and slide closer and closer to questionable practices that may still be legal. Sometimes maintaining high ethics is as easy as requesting that our managers ask a simple question when making a business decision: "Is this the right thing to do?" This may not always result in the best financial outcome in the short term, but it places ethical considerations at the center of the decision and does result in better financial outcomes over the long term. That is really what we are aiming for, to make ethics an integral part of the process.

Ethics is a long-term proposition. An entrepreneur has to be prepared to lose business in the short term. Early in our corporate history, I was approached by a number of influential lobbyists who said we could get contracts with the county and the city and a lot of money for our company in exchange for favors. We were not interested in obtaining contracts under those conditions and, therefore, lost the opportunity to do business with the government.

In the long run, we established ourselves as ethical players. This has had an obvious payback in our business. We are part of a young industry, susceptible to fraud. It has a lot of cash flow, low barriers to entry, little regulatory oversight and a long time between actions and consequences. I could have gone to Brazil with millions of dollars, and it would have been a year and a half before somebody had figured out what I had done.

When the time came for that founding group to lobby with legislators, our reputation as a group of principled companies in an industry that had a lot of dubious players really paid off. We had earned a lot of credibility, which helped create the industry and contributed to our business community.

Personally, it opened doors for me. It allowed me to convince the legislators and regulators that, even though we needed controls to keep unscrupulous operators from doing things their way, they should not kill our business. The PEO business makes a lot of sense. My partner, Pepe, likes to say, "If you do things right, if you do not cut corners, if you set a solid foundation, whether it be in family life or business, things will take care of themselves." I agree.

Epilogue

It is easy to look at a successful entrepreneur and say, "Boy, that's glamorous." It may look like overnight success, but the truth is that the 15 to 18 years that preceded that success were tough. Those of us who had corporate experience before starting our businesses could just as easily have gone in other directions. A thriving career in corporate America can mean generous compensation and, in many cases, highly interesting work.

When things get tough, as they were for us in the early years, they test one's resolve to stick with the idea. I think a combination of optimism and stubbornness is the key to success in entrepreneurial situations. I am a very optimistic person. I know I got that from my mother. Somehow, I always felt that we would do it, that we would make it. The stubbornness must be my own.

Those two attributes kept me going, but it was the challenge that drove it all. Pepe and I had a chance not only to create a business – challenging in itself – but also to help create a whole new industry. How often in a lifetime does one have an opportunity to do that?

The climate is different today. Our industry is huge and its potential for growth is tremendous. Vincam is one of the national leaders. We created and grew the company on a very simple premise: We would always seize the high road, take no short cuts and do things right. That earned us a sterling reputation within the industry. Even the industry's biggest critics will say that the one exception is Vincam. Pepe and I are proud of that, and we are even more proud of our reputation as a company that cares for its people. We like to say that Vincam is a company with a soul. We have a wonderful team of people here. They are a tremendous source of pride.

From a personal perspective, I think having four adult children who are fantastic human beings, who have great hearts and are law-abiding, respectful people, is my greatest source of pride, although 90 percent of the credit goes to Olga. I take pride in them and the lives they have built for themselves. They are my single biggest accomplishment.

Author's notes

Automatic Data Processing, Inc. (ADP) acquired the Vincam Group on March 11, 1999, for approximately 7.4 million shares of ADP common stock in a pooling of interest transaction. ADP, with over $4.5 billion in revenue and more than 425,000 clients, is one of the largest independent computing services firms in the world. Carlos Saladrigas was appointed CEO of ADP TotalSource (a division of ADP) on March 11, 1999.

Notes

[1] Yvonne M. Conde, *Operation Pedro Pan: The untold exodus of 14,000 Cuban children.* (New York: Routledge, Inc., 1999).

[2] Victor A. Triay, *Fleeing Castro: Operation Pedro Pan and the Cuban children's program.* (University Press of Florida, 1999).

CHAPTER NINE

Anna R. Cablik
*Setting Her Own Terms
in a Man's World*

ANATEK, INC.
ANASTEEL & SUPPLY CO. L.L.C.
ATLANTA, GEORGIA

ANATEK, INC.	ANASTEEL & SUPPLY CO. L.L.C.
Industry: Construction	Industry: Construction
Started: May 26, 1982	Started: April 1, 1994
Revenue: $6.5 million	Revenue: $ 9.3 million
Rate of Growth: 17%	Rate of Growth: -10%

Awards, Board Memberships and Accomplishments

1998 – 2000 Board Member, Georgia Chamber of Commerce,

1994 – 2000 Board Member, United Way

1997 Hispanic Business Woman of the Year,
United States Hispanic Chamber of Commerce

1997 Pacesetter Award. National Association
of Minority Contractors, Atlanta

1993 Minority Construction Firm of the Year,
U.S. Department of Commerce, Minority Business
Development Agency, Atlanta Region

I grew up on an isolated coffee and cattle farm in Panama. My parents were immigrants from Switzerland, and we spoke a dialect of German at home. I did not learn Spanish until I was six years old, in the first grade. We all worked that farm and, as farms go, we worked like slaves. Growing up, I decided that once I left the farm, I would never return.

Through fifth grade I went to a village school, and rode an hour on horseback to get there. During the rainy season, the noon rains were especially bad. The streams would get so high, that we couldn't cross on horseback. Whenever there was a big rain, the teachers would let us go home early. I remember many times the water was up to my horse's saddle. It did not seem so risky at the time, but it was.

Looking back, it seems that under some circumstances, people take a lot more risks. I guess that's something I have carried with me all my life. When I compare my risk tolerance with my husband's, I take about six times more risk than he does.

That school closed after I finished fifth grade, and for a year my mother tutored my sister and me at home. We studied math and Spanish, even though my mother's Spanish was not the greatest.

When I was 12 years old, I went to a Catholic boarding school. Technically, I never really graduated from sixth grade since I was studying at home during that time. But, I was so adamant not to repeat sixth grade that the nuns relented and said I could begin the seventh grade. If I could not keep up with the work, however, I would have to go back to the sixth grade.

I went to work that year knowing that I would be first in my class. That school – all schools in Panama, for that matter – had a ranking system. My sister, who had gone to school a year earlier, was ranked second. She was a hardworking student; yet, that first place remained elusive. I told my sister, "When I go to school, I will be first in my class." My mind was made up, and it was as good as done.

When I started seventh grade, my biggest challenge was English. I had never studied English, and the other children had studied it from the first grade. I was at a serious disadvantage going in, but I was not going to settle for anything less than that first place.

The boarding school was very regimented. Lights went out at 8 p.m. That was a problem because it cut back my study time. But I figured I could study in the bathroom because the lights were on all night. I got acquainted with Dick and Jane and Spot sitting on the floor of that bathroom. I managed to be at the top of my class from that first semester on, and eventually graduated valedictorian.

College Years

I dreamed of being a nuclear physicist and I applied to colleges in the United States, including the University of Houston. I wanted to work for NASA. I was accepted at the University of Houston but without a scholarship. I was also accepted at other colleges, all without scholarships, except at the Canal Zone Junior College, which was a U.S. government-operated junior college. I couldn't afford to go without a scholarship, so I enrolled there. It was not in the United States, but it was a step in the right direction.

The Canal Zone Junior College was a two-year college. Its only four-year program was in medical technology. My parents, being practical people, told me to take the four-year program because "there's just no money to be frittering around and not getting anywhere."

With my usual optimism, I became a student of medical technology and everything else I could squeeze into my schedule. Squeeze I did. I took almost all the courses the college offered, in addition to the requirements for medical technician.

The State Department's scholarship paid my tuition. The Panamanian government also offered a scholarship to the top three children in every school in the nation. My determination and competitive spirit paid off. The scholarship included a $100-a-month stipend. My parents paid for the dormitory, $90 dollars a semester for a room.

I was set – except for food. The dormitory did not have a cafeteria, so food was up to us. As a Panamanian in the Canal Zone, I was not able to buy from local groceries, because they were for Americans only. I had to go to Panama to purchase groceries, and since I didn't have a vehicle, I was dependent on my friends to buy my food.

During my sophomore year, I met my future husband who worked for the federal government as a civilian in the Canal Zone. I met him at one of those matchmaking parties where they matched soldiers with local girls. The party was at my teacher's house. I don't remember who took me, but when I needed to go home, I didn't have a ride. My teacher asked my future husband to give me a ride home.

We dated for three years. We were good friends, and he took me out to eat often. Pretty much, he fed me through college. I graduated on June 30, 1974. We were married six days later.

Not long after that, my husband was offered a job as an Army manpower analyst in Atlanta. We moved in October 1974. The job required a lot of travel. He was gone as much as six weeks at a time.

From Medical Technician
to Construction

The day we arrived in Atlanta, my husband left on assignment. I didn't know a soul. All our money was in traveler's checks, and I didn't have a driver's license or a credit card. I had a hard time getting stores or the bank to accept my traveler's checks. Buying groceries was a problem again. The only identification I had was my green card. I was so frustrated, I told my husband I wanted to go back to Panama because "these people are treating me like dirt." I felt stranded in Atlanta.

The first thing I did was to apply for a job at Piedmont Hospital, and the first thing they did was to ask if I had passed my certification. I had taken the test in the Canal Zone but didn't have the results yet. They didn't believe me at first, because the medical technology students in Atlanta who had taken their tests at the same time already had received their results. They asked me to come back as soon as I got my results. A couple of week later, I got my results and they hired me right away. I started working the evening shift, 3 to 11 p.m.

I found myself with a lot of time on my hands. My husband was traveling, and we didn't have children. An elderly couple who lived in our apartment building took a liking to me. The woman's son had just started a business on the ground floor of the building. Once, in passing, I mentioned to her how I had squeezed so much into my academic schedule that I had a secretarial certificate as well. Her son needed part-time help during the week, and that is how I got into construction.

From Secretary to Vice President

You could say I had some experience. I had a job in the Canal Zone after I graduated from high school typing specifications for facility engineers. Yet, it was serendipitous that I ended up in construction. I immediately fell in love with this job.

Hard work was part of my nature from the very start. I was always a very driven person. In Panama, while working for the facility engineers, I typed twice as fast as anybody else. The other secretaries would get mad and ask, "Why do you work so hard? You don't need to work so hard." I would answer, "I get my work done. Then if I don't have anything to do, I goof off; but I'm not going to just goof off for the sake of goofing off."

Hard work has always paid off for me. I believe it is the reason I was able to move up so quickly, and why my companies have done so well.

I worked for the construction company a couple of hours every other day. Eventually, the business became bigger, and I ended up working from 8 a.m. until noon every day. That was fine until my schedule at the hospital changed to ten-hour shifts, from 1 to 11 p.m. Soon, it got so I just couldn't keep up. As the last shift, we had to do the routine work so the graveyard shift, 11 p.m. to 7 a.m., wouldn't have to deal with anything except emergencies.

I was getting home at 2 o'clock in the morning and back at work at eight. I resigned from my day job but offered to stay on until they found a replacement. A week later the owner offered to pay what I was making at the hospital. That meant I wouldn't have to work evenings or be on call. That decision was easy – I went to work for him full time.

The company bought and resold construction materials, which involved a tremendous amount of paperwork. African-American and Caucasian partners owned the company, and one of their major customers was MARTA, the mass transportation system in Atlanta. The owners were out most of the time, so I was the only person left in the office. This provided the best learning opportunity I could wish for, and I learned the business quickly.

When customers called and asked something I didn't know, I took down information and called them back after I figured out what was happening. I started out as a clerk. Seven years later I was vice president with total administrative responsibility. I was in charge of making sure we had money to pay for everything and enough work to keep the crews busy. The office staff had grown to eight by then, and we had 20 people in the field placing reinforcing rods, working the sawmill and the metal fabrication shop. I worked directly with the shop superintendent and the foreman. The only thing I did not do was to supervise the crews. I learned that later on.

... A Piece of the Pie?

As part of my job, I worked closely with one of our most important contractors in New York. The company's chief estimator came to Atlanta often and I was responsible for taking him to lunch and dinner. He helped put things in perspective. He brought things to my attention that I had not thought about. He would say, "You must have a pretty good piece of the pie over there." I thought to myself, "Piece of the pie? I don't have a piece of the pie."

He would add, "Well, you must be getting really good pay over there, the way you work ..." I was very dedicated and never slacked off. One day it really sank in. He said, "I've got a secretary that I pay $22,000 a year. All she does is answer my phone, make sure I get my messages straight and take care of whatever I need to do." I was making about $18,000. I knew that salaries were higher in New York than in Atlanta, but I could no longer ignore the difference between my responsibility and my salary.

Coincidentally, some friction developed between me and one of the owners. I was responsible for running the office, but if I made a decision that he didn't like, suddenly I was just a clerk. He would come back and chastise me: "Why did you do this?" and "Why did you do that?" I would say, "Well, you're never here to make a decision. I can't wait for the 11th hour to make a decision."

My frustration was building. I had my child in day care that was halfway between my home and my office. The traffic in Atlanta is very heavy in the morning. I took my child in as early as I was allowed. He was usually the first one there. It took me an hour to get to my office. Most of the time I would make it on time, but once in a while I would be about five minutes late. On those few days when I walked in two or three minutes after eight, the one boss would say, "Good evening, Mrs. Cablik." That grated on my nerves, because I worked like a slave. I didn't go to the bathroom half the time, I never took lunch and I often stayed late.

The office became more and more uncomfortable. I told my husband that I didn't know how much longer I was going to stay. I loved my job – I really enjoyed what I was doing – but I just couldn't deal with the way the one owner treated me. He was a "throw a fit, slam the doors and cuss" kind of boss.

The straw that broke the camel's back happened on Monday, April 12, 1982. The boss had requested production forecast and cash flow projections late the previous Friday afternoon, so late that I could not delegate the work. He wanted the report completed by 11 a.m. Monday. That meant I had to do it myself. I took all that stuff home, and over the weekend my husband and I worked on that darned thing. I stayed up all night Sunday and finished the report by 5 o'clock Monday morning. I was exhausted and frustrated.

That morning as I was dropping off my four-year-old son at day care, he turned and said, "Mommy, this car is not yours, is it?" I said, "No, honey, this is not my car." "Well if you ever quit your job you would have to give this car back." "Yes, honey, I would."

It was prophetic.

I had everything ready for the 11 o'clock meeting. We started with the January cash flow projections. I had a projection that was very close to the actual and they were very happy with it. However, the February projection was off by $15,000, which in construction is not unusual. I thought I had done a pretty good job of projecting figures, but the one owner just had a conniption and told me to go back to my office and twiddle my thumbs. I offered my resignation on the spot. He wanted it immediately in writing, so I gave it to him.

I had to turn in my company car, so I couldn't get home. I didn't dare ask the people in the office for a ride, because he would have fired them for helping me. So I waited until they got off work and asked one of the engineers to take me home.

I was very upset. It puzzled me for a long time. I had helped build the company. At first I really loved the company, and they treated me very well, but at the end it was totally adversarial. I loved my job but I hated to go in. Loyalty and hard work sometimes don't count.

Looking back, I think there were several issues. The son of one of the owners worked at the company. I cannot help think the owner wanted him to have my position, so he probably was just trying to make me quit.

Another reason may have contributed. The partners had approached me to set up a woman-owned company with them. I would own 60 percent of that company, but I was not to have control over it. My response was, "If I own 60 percent, I'm going to control 60 percent." When I said that, the deal was over.

As I thought about what I would do next, I did not realize the wheels were already in motion. I had been the point of contact for all the contractors who called the office. When they asked for me and I wasn't there, they were shocked.

When I left, I told one of the engineers that if anybody asked for me to give them my home number. Within three days I had received seven job offers. I took two weeks off to do things around the house and get myself together before taking on something new.

We had just bought a new house and had all these bills. I couldn't just sit at home, even though my husband had a good job. Most of the offers I got were for more money than I had been making, even though the people who offered thought it was less.

The Business Ownership Option

I made up my mind that I would go to work for the contractor from New York. Then I got a call from the chief estimator: "I know they offered you a job, but don't take it." I said, "What do you mean? "

He said, "You need to open your own business. You're a minority. You're Hispanic, you're female. You have literally been running the business for them. Go and open your own business." I said, "Sure, with luck. I don't have any money to open a business."

"As a minority, you're able to negotiate certain things," he said. "You know what's going on; you are experienced. Consider it and don't take the job. Because if you do, should you decide later to go out on your own, you couldn't do business with us because it would be a conflict of interest."

"Why don't you just work as a consultant for a while until you decide whether you want to go out on your own?"

Entrepreneurship, What Do We Have to Lose?

So I started working as a consultant doing estimates. I talked it over with my husband, and I said, "What do we have to lose?" Well, we had a lot to lose. If I didn't make it, it was a second income we didn't have. Finally, about a month later, we said we would give it a try. We would have to tighten our belts and deal with a little bit less. My humble beginnings came in very handy.

Once we decided we were going into business, I used $500 dollars to incorporate. I started working out of my house bidding work. My first contract, from the company in New York, was a cost-plus arrangement. What a blessing!

It gave me two opportunities. It was a first job. When asked about experience, I could refer customers to this job. My first contract, for $2 million, was to do all the steelwork at MARTA's Lakewood Station. We did the reinforcing steel, the structural steel and all miscellaneous steelwork, including the handrails and the telephone cabinets. Anything that had to do with steel, we did it.

The second benefit was that it was a cost-plus, which meant we didn't lose any money. We didn't make any either, but it gave me the opportunity to go out on my own and find out what was out there. The company was honest and straightforward and gave me good references.

I was able to get a lot more jobs as a result of this first contract. I started building the company. Anatek, Inc., was on her way.

Initially, there were a lot of surprises. I was now working directly with the ironworkers. I had a big eye-opener early on. I had hired several men for an important job. The next day, one of the guys wasn't there. "Where's so-and-so?" I asked. The answer came back so casually: "Oh, he's in jail."

In jail? I almost died. I had never dealt with anybody who had been in jail. To them, this was no big deal. Then the FBI came and told me some employees were dealing cocaine on my job. The FBI wanted to put a secret agent on my job. I was shocked. The drug dealer turned out to be my superintendent. I was even more shocked.

I finished the job ahead of schedule and within budget. My goal was to prove I was able to do the job. When I opened my business, the talk on the street was, "Oh, yeah, that stupid woman. Give her some time – she will hang herself in six months." Little did they know they were fueling my determination to succeed. Fortunately, my first job lasted over a year and a half, almost two years. So much for that.

Anatek, Inc.

Anatek, Inc., started out as a distributor. Now it's a steel erector. I do some general contracting, but our strength is doing the steelwork or anything that has to do with metal – structural support and beams for bridges. We erect structural steel beams as well as concrete beams.

My business started as a union shop. It was a requirement on my first contract. It was great, because the union was a good source of trained labor. After completing my first job, I branched out and started working on highways. Eventually I was doing more highway projects than anything else. I quickly found that I could not compete, because the highway industry in Atlanta is totally non-union. For several months I didn't get any highway work. One of the contractors told me that if I really wanted to get highway work, I needed to get out of the union.

I set up a new company, made that one non-union and left Anatek as a union company. The same contractor suggested that representing a union and non-union companies was going to get me into trouble. I talked it over with my lawyer, and he agreed. So I got to where I didn't have any work. I didn't renew my agreement with the union, and then I started over.

I closed the company in May 1985 and started another company with the same name in September.

I didn't pay myself a salary for three years. Even though my first job was a cost-plus project, the cost-plus was so small I could not afford to pay myself. I had a trailer and a telephone at the job site. I had a vehicle and paid my gas. The only reason I was able to survive was that my husband had a steady income. For many years, we did not even run the air-conditioning in our house, because we just couldn't afford it. It took a lot of determination and a lot of sacrifice.

Then I got pregnant again. It wasn't exactly planned. For a long time I didn't tell anybody, until I couldn't hide it any more. Of course, everybody gave me a hard time. My biggest problem was child care. I was hoping my in-laws would take care of the baby until the child-care center could take him at six weeks, but they felt it was too much responsibility. I had no choice: I took him to work. It worked well. He was an excellent baby. People thought I was odd and crazy, but they accepted my determination.

I remember one time I had to negotiate a change order with a contractor and the owners. Remember, this is construction, a very male-dominated industry. I brought my baby with me in a little carrier. I put him next to me on the floor and business went on as usual. When he was old enough for child care, he joined his brother.

When I could afford to pay myself a salary, it wasn't really that much. Fortunately, over the years, as I did a lot better and got more contracts, I was able to increase my salary. When I was certified under the minority program, I was able to partner with organizations that had secured government contracts. Since they were required to have minority subcontractors they contacted me. That was the only reason some businesses would give me the work, reality being as it is. The minority program forces contractors to look beyond the people they would normally feel comfortable with. As my reputation for dependability grew, I got a lot of customers who didn't even need a minority (contractor).

I have never been a Small Business Administration 8A company. I was certified as a minority in the state of Georgia. At the beginning I qualified as an 8A, but the paperwork was so mind-boggling that I never bothered. Right now I couldn't qualify – too big.

Finding My Niche Market

I discovered my market niche over time. It was a combination of circumstances, some of which I did not like at the time, and a little serendipity. Once I had identified my niche, it helped define the business and my potential growth strategy.

I started Anatek in 1982 because the highway construction industry was a good place to be. There were two or three other reinforcing steel placers just like us. Over the years many companies have started in this industry. But right now, I am the only minority-owned reinforcing steel placer in the Southeast that has been in business for more than three years, and the only minority-owned steel fabricator.

At Anatek, Inc., we work mostly with highway contractors and general contractors who work for public agencies like the EPA. We seldom work directly with a customer. We are a subcontractor. On occasion we will work as the general contractor; for instance, we won a fairly large contract – almost $2 million – for the Olympics.

Bonding is a big deal in construction. For many years, even after Anatek became a profitable company, the bonding companies refused to bond me. They have a magic formula that you have to have a certain amount of working capital to be able to do a certain volume of work. I never had enough working capital, so according to them I could not possibly make it in the business. I was making it, but I didn't fit their formula, their mold.

I was able to work without bonding because of the minority rule. Even subcontractors must be bonded on jobs of $10,000 or more. However, because general contractors had to meet a certain goal for minorities, they were willing to waive the bond requirement. My first job, my cost-plus job, did not require a bond. Since I finished the job on time and within budget, I could encourage contractors to waive the bond on future jobs.

But without a bond, I could not be a general contractor. I was condemned to be a subcontractor. The bonding requirements determined my size, my customer and my niche. Fortunately, it all worked out in the end.

Over the years, I grew the company to about 120 employees and about $13 million in revenue. That was an important lesson. I found that bigger is not necessarily better. Even though I did a lot more volume, I was losing money. I figured I was better off doing less work and having better control. I decided my market niche was a sales volume of $6 or $7 million.

Once we discovered that Anatek had an optimum size, growth meant expanding through acquisition.

Growth Through Acquisition

I purchased Anasteel in April of 1994. The business was not doing well; it was competing against fabricators who were owned by the mills. I entered as a majority partner. I kept the same business, but I established a niche and increased production. These changes made the company profitable.

Anasteel is an independent fabricator. We buy steel from the mills. Some of those mills also have their own fabricators. Consequently, we are both a customer and a competitor, which puts us in a peculiar position. The mills that have their own fabricating shops determine what kind of jobs we get. Even with minority requirements, we cannot compete on large projects — projects over 1,000 tons of reinforcing steel. Fabricators that have their own mills always be less expensive than we are. To beat their prices, I would have to give away the steel. The mills do not have to make money at the fabrication level. For these reasons, the larger projects simply were not worth my time.

So, we concentrate on the small jobs that big fabricators don't want to fool with. Our niche is in part determined by the nature of large jobs and the companies that bid them. Big companies have backlogs that will keep them busy for a while. Our backlog is never very high. So we can accommodate customers who need steel next week. On the other hand, the big guys with the big jobs have full schedules, and cannot accommodate customers who need quick turnaround.

In addition, we can charge prime rates because of the quick turnaround. In essence, we can make more money on the small jobs than on the big ones.

Future growth and expansion will probably follow this path. We will invest in some companies, and will purchase others. In time, we may be a conglomerate of small companies in the construction industry. It all depends on other, more important circumstances, such as family and enjoying life. These fall into the greater definition of expansion, growth and success.

That's The Business

I've been in business 16 years. I've had very bad years and very good years. Experience has taught me that if my competitors equal, fall below or just barely exceed my cost, they can have the work. That's not arrogance, that's business.

People ask me, if I were to do it over, would I? Quite frankly, I might go into a different business. This industry is extremely demanding. You have many challenges, high risks and very low returns. The profit margins in construction range from 1 to 3 percent. If you are lucky, you hit five. The start-up issues with bonding and insurance, exposure, and the risks in employee safety, lawsuits or something going wrong are very, very high.

Challenges are a daily occurrence in this business. It takes a lot of energy and a lot of management skills to get something like this going. I truly feel that if I had taken all my energy, my enthusiasm and my management skills to another industry, I could have made a lot more money.

I have survived and succeeded in this industry because I am persistent and I take reasonable risks. Like most entrepreneurs, I have a stomach for a lot of risk. Otherwise, I would not have made it. I go out on a limb and believe that the limb is not going to break, but I choose healthy limbs, not rotten or weak ones.

I believe my competitive advantage right now is that I do what I say I'm going to do. I deliver. That is key to me. I do not mislead people in any way. I'm very up-front. Many times I will get the job, even when I'm not the low bidder.

Bonding and Insurance

Bonding is a measure of substance. Therefore, if you can bond, it means there is some substance to your business. If you cannot bond, it means you have a problem. That is why contractors who know that you can bond won't require it. Today, I tell them I can bond but they have to pay for it. They don't want to pay the extra money, and they figure if you can bond, you're strong enough to get the job done. It helps that I've been in business 16 years. The chances of going under now are less than when I had been in business for only two or three years.

I had the same experience with insurance. When I first tried to get insurance, nobody would give it to me. I had no track record, and insurance companies will not insure start-ups. I added, "How in the world do I get past start-up if you don't give me insurance when I'm starting?" Eventually, I found an agent who, for whatever reason, believed in me. I was operating out of my house at the time. To this day, he's my agent. He gets first refusal for my business. At least 10 insurance companies want my business now. I pay a lot of money in insurance. When you consider all insurance – health, worker's compensation, and life – I pay close to $250,000 a year just for Anatek.

Getting Sued

Getting sued is part of doing business. I sometimes consider it an operational cost. When you start a business, everybody knows you don't have anything so everybody leaves you alone. But the minute you have two nickels, 10 people want them.

The most frustrating lawsuit was a liability suit. We were working the bridge over Interstate 285, the beltway around Atlanta. It is a huge expressway with six 12-foot lanes both ways. We were subcontractors.

The contractor placed barriers to divert traffic away from the construction site near the new pier in the middle of I-285.

A pickup truck swerved and hit one of these barriers and knocked it over. The barrier fell into the road, probably two feet into the outside lane. Which left 10 feet of lane to drive around the barrier. A car came along, with another following close behind. The first driver swerved around the barrier, but the second driver didn't see it in time and ran into it.

After the accident, the police interviewed one of my workers. The next thing I knew, I was being sued. The suit said we were liable. The driver was suing us for everything because she couldn't be a companion to her husband. When I first got the suit, I said, "These people are crazy. I didn't have anything to do with that barrier." As subcontractors, we did not put the barrier there. We didn't have any control over the barrier.

At that time, they weren't even suing the general contractor. Amazing. My contract clearly said that all traffic control was the responsibility of the general contractor. We ended up going before a jury. By the time we got to court there were three defendants, because they had then brought the general contractor into the lawsuit. So there was the general contractor, the insurance company and us.

We settled for $120,000 before the final verdict, because we were afraid that the jury would award the woman more than my insurance coverage. I learned that when you go to court, the best attorney wins. We tried to get out of the lawsuit altogether. The prevailing opinion was that we had a duty to the traveling public to protect them from accidents.

The lawyer's fees at that point, after three years of very little litigation, was $60,000. In general, my philosophy is, settle any dispute without attorneys. Lawyers will get their share regardless of outcome. They don't guarantee anything. I guess I am not a fan of litigation. Sometimes lawyers can help keep you from making a mistake, like my issue with setting up the two companies. Lawyers are good for planning.

Overcoming Challenges

Dark days abound in my industry. One of my darkest days came in 1988, when the company was highly profitable. I was still paying myself a pretty low salary. I didn't have any equity or collateral because of the way Anatek was set up. Assets were always a big issue. So, the only way I could build assets was to leave the money in the company. We didn't have a lot of equipment, we didn't own land.

The prior year had ended well and it was looking like another great year. But, I one of my contractors who was seriously delinquent in paying us for work we had already completed. This was a problem, because we report taxes on the percent completed. The contractor owed $300,000. I was about to run out of my bond. I had tried to get these guys to pay me, but their company was in serious trouble. Attorneys I consulted felt I had a pretty good case. The day I told the contractor I was going to file a lien against the bond, the owner of the company called and told me he was willing to send me a certified check for $250,000 to settle the whole thing.

I was tempted to settle, because cash flow was one of my biggest problems, but the attorneys were against it. They told me they could get half a million dollars. So I told the guy I was not willing to settle. Just after I told him – and I was really pinched for cash – I got my tax return. I owed $267,000 in income tax. Fortunately, I had a line of credit with the bank. I borrowed every dime to pay my taxes. I paid my taxes and squeaked by from week to week to pay my payroll of $25,000 to $30,000 a week.

While I was recovering from that situation, one day I opened my mail and found a notice from the bank that I had to pay out my line of credit. I broke out in a cold sweat. You only pay out your line of credit once a year and I had just opened it to pay for taxes. I collected myself and called the bank. It turned out to be a mistake. I said, "Well, if you want me to pay it, I'll do it." I did not know where I would get the money, but I would find it if I had to. They said, "No, no. Don't worry about it."

Talk about being saved by the bell! I almost fainted. I was thrilled when I was finally able to pay off the line of credit. Fortunately, I have accumulated some of my own money now for these kinds of emergencies.

An Entrepreneur and a Woman Entrepreneur

I did not see myself as an entrepreneur during the early years. I was doing what an entrepreneur does, but I was doing it with an employee mindset. It took me a while to develop that strong entrepreneurial personality. You could say I was a late-blooming entrepreneur. I had not thought about owning a company until that New York contractor's chief estimator planted the seed. That is the first time it occurred to me that I could be doing for myself what I was doing for others.

Today, I am very clear about who I am. I am an entrepreneur because I am willing to go out, start a business, take the risk and do what it takes to make it a success.

Much of the entrepreneurial experience is common to both men and women entrepreneurs. For instance, each of us has to deal with gauging and seizing opportunity, taking risks and figuring out how to grow our business. But ultimately, entrepreneurship is an individual experience. We must figure out how to deal with those common entrepreneurial challenges from the vantage point of who we are and what we bring to the experience. What I bring to my entrepreneurial experience as a Hispanic woman of Swiss descent in a male society – which construction has been – is a mixture that has worked well for me. My experience has had a unique set of challenges and, within those challenges, opportunities.

I was part of the opportunity mix when I considered starting the company. I was experienced, and I had know-how and connections in the industry. Most importantly, I knew that my commitment in the form of sweat equity and my willingness to put in the time and effort necessary were my greatest opportunity assets. I don't believe in failure. To me, the words "cannot do" or "impossible" don't exist. Once I determine that I'm going to do something, I do it. This is especially true when people tell me I cannot do it. This has been a definite asset.

The rest I learned as I went along. I learned, for instance, to trust my instincts. Fortunately, the good Lord was watching out for me as I grew along with my businesses and tried to figure it all out. Several times I have postponed making an important decision, finding out later that it was the best thing I could have done. Sometimes when I don't get a great job, I say, "The best job is the one I didn't get." More than once, as it turned out, that was exactly so. Not exactly good planning, but something just didn't feel right. Those great jobs turned out to be bitter lemons for the companies that were "fortunate" enough to get them. My gut feelings have been assets in this business.

I also learned to use my strengths. I had a good background in bookkeeping. My books are essential to my operation in which margins are so small. If I had not had this skill,
I would have hired someone immediately, because this is
essential to making it in this industry.

I consider speaking Spanish another competitive advantage. I probably have been very Americanized in many ways.
Number one, I'm impressed with the fact that in the United
States, a woman is able to do what I did. In Panama, it would
be almost impossible. There, a man does "man things" and a
woman does work that is for women. I give a lot of credit to
my husband, who was willing to support me and to work
more with the kids at home. But I recognize that my language and culture have been instrumental in my success.

I am still working on the unique problems that being a
woman brings to running and growing my businesses. For
instance, I have had a problem finding somebody who
would take care of business and not resent working for a
woman. This is especially so at Anatek: I have hired several
men in the last five to six years, but I'm back to running it all
myself. One manager who was working out very well suddenly quit. I was shocked and asked him why. I was happy
with him and was paying him very well. He said he resent-
ed the fact I was getting paid more than him and that I was
undermining his authority. Basically he did not feel comfortable working for a woman. I probably wouldn't hire another
man, or perhaps I would hire somebody younger. I don't
think the older generation deals very well with women in
leadership roles.

I guess I am a pretty tough person to work for. I expect a
lot of people, because I do a lot myself. I have been able to
make money in a demanding industry where I have seen too
many people unable to make it.

I figured it was going to be tough because the mentality of
a lot of the contractors is that a woman belongs in the
kitchen, barefoot and pregnant. They gave me a hard time

and I had to prove myself over and over. I proved to them that I was willing to do the work, take responsibility for fixing my errors and do whatever it takes to succeed. The industry eventually did bestow upon me some measure of respect. That's how I was able to succeed where a lot of other people didn't. My opportunity asset gained me respect in an industry where women "just did not belong."

Partnership

I am the majority partner in each of my companies. I am most satisfied with the partnership at Anasteel. My partner is an active partner, who owns 49 percent of the company. The reason this partnership works is that each of us brings strengths to benefit the company, we both contribute to the business and we respect each other.

This partnership emerged from a standing business relationship. Anatek was buying steel from the firm, and the owner approached me about buying the business. He had been losing money for a while. He was very honest. He told me I could look at any documents and ask questions. He didn't hide anything from me.

It appeared the issue was production. The company couldn't get enough production to make a profit. I talked with the employees. The superintendent gave me a hard time, but the rest of the people on the floor told me that production could be increased. After looking under every rock, I believed I could turn the company around by working with the workers. I convinced myself it could be done.

I told the owner I would be willing to go into it, but I could invest only a limited amount of money. He looked at my offer and decided that it was enough to make the deal work. I was adamant that to best manage this firm, I had to be the majority partner. I think this was hard on him, but eventually he agreed.

I no longer believe in silent partners. Partnership to me means that each person adds value to the organization and complements the other's strengths and weaknesses.

Partnerships evolve, just as companies grow and people develop. When you're down and out and don't have anything, it's easy to give away a lot. When you have nothing, 50 percent of nothing is still nothing. If you have a partner who isn't going to work side by side with you, sooner or later it will stop being a good partnership. In looking for a partner, I now make sure that the person will add value daily to the partnership and to the company and can continue to do so for a long time.

Right now I have a buy/sell agreement with my partners. If something were to happen to me, they would take over the company. My husband doesn't want any part of it. As time passes and my kids get older, that might change. The buy/sell agreement at Anasteel has been in effect from the start.

The one at Anatek went into effect in 1990. I was more or less pushed into it by the bonding company, which gets very nervous about being stuck with a company if a key player leaves. Right now I'm kind of stuck with an agreement I don't like. I probably will let it expire and not renew it, perhaps try to buy out my partner. That's a big issue when you work with a partner.

One of the things I tell people when I encourage them to start their own businesses is to look far ahead and ask what kind of percentage they would be willing to give a partner if their company were worth $10 million.

Success and Growth

When I started, my goal was to be worth $1 million by the time I was 40. I started when I was 30. As far as volume goes, I pictured myself doing maybe a couple of million dollars a year. But the profit margins in this industry are a lot smaller than I had anticipated. Sometimes I dream of becoming a multimillion-dollar corporation, but I realize that to do that, I would have to get more people to work with me.

I'm not sure I want to do that. There are other options; for instance, I might get involved with other companies. I could decide to buy them or invest in them instead of actually running them.

When I started, I dreamed of becoming as successful as I am today. When I visit Panama, my people ask if I'm satisfied where I am. I tell them that it is relative. When I look at myself now, compared with where I came from, I am very wealthy. When I compare myself with Rockefeller, I'm still poor. The real question is not how wealthy I can become or how much will satisfy me, but how much am I willing to sacrifice to satisfy ambition.

For instance, my husband is retired and is looking forward to doing something besides watching me leave for work at seven in the morning and getting home at eight at night. When you want to enjoy other things in life besides running a business, you have to make choices.

Realistically, I could be a multi-millionaire. I'm not that old yet. But how willing am I to hang in there? I think it all depends on how you define success. I believe I'm successful. I felt successful when I reached my first goal of having $1 million. I then set other goals and have met them also. I guess it is easy to keep seeking more, the more you have. It is probably a part of that natural trend of needing to grow and develop – or maybe you get greedy as you get more.

You get used to a certain lifestyle, and then you're not willing to have less. Not that you can't do with less. I don't think I would have a hard time going back to living with a lot less, but I think my family would have a really rough time. On the other hand, what does it all mean, if I do not have the time to fully enjoy it? This is a dilemma for me right now, which probably will become more pressing with time.

There are quality-of-life issues around the mechanics of growing a company as well. How big do I want to get, and what does size have to do with anything? Growing from 1 to 25 employees in three months wasn't that big of an issue, because my payroll was being covered on a weekly basis with the cost-plus arrangement. I was in the union. I called the union hall and told them how many people I needed, and they sent them out. That part was easy.

Later on, however, I got in trouble when I grew from doing $8 million to $13 million. I was managing 120 employees, along with other issues like contractors who weren't paying on time or at all. I had three people in the office; right now, there are only two. I had 14 crews; now I have eight or nine. My crews were larger – maybe 10 or 12 people. Now they are four or five people. The number of employees multiplied the issues of payroll, attendance, mistakes and scheduling. It was mind-boggling. I learned that bigger is not necessarily better, and that sometimes you can be more profitable doing less rather than more. The pleasures of life are priceless, and it is more important to define success by those standards than just by business standards and accumulating wealth.

Epilogue

A successful entrepreneur is one who makes the most of opportunities, faces challenges, uses intuition, knows business and the business, has a growth strategy and takes smart risks. A successful partnership is one in which all partners are actively involved in adding value to the company on a daily basis, which evolves with the company's needs. A successful person reaches goals but knows what price to pay for success.

PART III

LESSONS AND LEGACIES FOR THE NEW MILLENIUM

CHAPTER TEN

LEADERSHIP LESSONS AND BEST PRACTICES

These three concluding chapters are about the leadership of these six entrepreneurs, the legacy they are helping to build and how it all ties together. Using their life experiences, these six entrepreneurs have assembled the elements of their personal lives and businesses to produce a natural synergy for growth. The result is a winning combination of talents, skills and successes that is unique to each individual.

With time and a tremendous amount of hard work, they have produced fast-growth businesses. They seem to have done this by knowing their strengths, weaknesses and preferences and by doing the "right things" in business, with family and for community. Their stories prove there is no one way to do this, for the parts of each successful combination overlap, complement each other and merge, defying attempts to find specific formulas.

It is easy to suggest that these six entrepreneurs could have been successful in any field they would have selected. They are talented, intelligent and resourceful people – so why choose entrepreneurship and why pursue high growth?

Perhaps their personal affinity for growth may have attracted them to entrepreneurial opportunities. Other interesting and challenging options might not have provided the type and scale of growth that feels most comfortable to these entrepreneurs.

While each participant's process of fast growth entrepreneurship is highly personal, there are four leadership practices that they believe helped them as entrepreneurs and businesspeople and that may be useful to others seeking to put together their own winning combination. These four leadership practices are interrelated and create the setting for growth to occur. They include:

- Setting the vision and the three C's
- Growing
- Learning
- Teaming

Setting the Vision and the Three C's

Vision and the three C's – customer service, communication and culture – are the leadership characteristics these entrepreneurs felt were their most immediate and important responsibilities. They believe that when these work together, they create a competitive advantage not easily replicated by others.

Vision

Vision is a picture of the future. It describes possibility. It is an intangible force that moves, motivates and creates action to overcome challenges. It imparts conviction, a sense of responsibility, optimism and spirit to founding or growing a business, an industry or a community. As mentioned earlier, in Spanish, *visión*, with its strong emphasis on the last syllable, connotes determination as well as ambition and, sometimes, a sense of urgency. Thus the word gives a sense of strength and importance.

The six entrepreneurs are people of vision, of *visión*. Their convictions about what they wanted their futures to be were always firm. Yet, as practical and savvy businesspeople, their visions tended to include a realism that comes from experience. What is truly amazing is their common vision to build something of consequence, not just to be successful businesspeople. It is almost as if they were building a legacy that will make a significant and lasting difference for others.

Each of the six developed his or her personal vision in childhood and changed it as they matured. Danny initially was looking for his "ticket." As a young adult, he changed his vision to one of a thriving community, of quality education and of real opportunities for the less fortunate. This has not changed.

Nancy imagined flying among the stars, a life of stability for herself and her children, and finally building a successful and humane company and an equally successful community.

As a child, Tom looked forward to a better life and a career in music. As a successful senior executive, he changed that vision to one of starting and leading an organization that engenders scientific creativity.

Anna envisioned academic and career excellence. Later that changed to business and community excellence.

When Carlos was a child, he worked hard to achieve self-sufficiency for himself and his parents. As an adult, he envisioned a highly successful business within an equally successful industry that provided the highest value-added services so other entrepreneurial businesses could realize their own visions. His vision expanded to include an ethical government and business community and quality education and health care for all.

Teresa visualized a community of diversity in which difference was not just tolerated but valued. This vision grew into that of a fast-growth company that values the contributions of all associates.

Customer Service

Great customer service is achieved when all the aspects of organizational growth come together correctly. These entrepreneurs built their companies for it; they planned for it and they modeled it. Interestingly, they advocate that customer service is to a great extent about ethics, and believe that successful entrepreneurs communicate this consistently.

Both Nancy and Tom returned significant amounts of money they did not need for government contracts they had worked on, money that could make a huge difference in a start-up operation's bottom line. Yet, they felt strongly that this was the right thing to do. It fit with how they chose to do business – ethically and fairly. Coincidentally, these expressions of their values significantly affected their organizations' cultures. The return of money became part of company folklore and has remained a source of pride as these decisions created future business opportunities with the government agencies to which they originally returned the money.

The tremendous growth Vincam experienced is based on satisfied customers. The economies of scale, scope, distribution and focus represent solid business practices to Carlos. But they are much more: They allow Vincam to provide specialized services to its customers who could not otherwise afford them. This enables customers, many of whom are also entrepreneurs, to attract and retain experienced and talented employees. Carlos remarks:

> We focus on retention. Our economies of scale, scope, distribution and focus work are based on the notion that we keep our customers for a long time. It is more profitable to provide exceptional customer service and to further develop products and services our current customers can use than to acquire new customers. In fact, new customers are very expensive. We barely cover initial expenses with new customers. Therefore, everybody in the company is

focused on retention. It is everybody's job to take care clients, regardless of when they call or how the client got to you.

Carlos believes that most business decisions have ethical implications and makes sure that Vincam's leadership asks questions about ethics as it manages daily operations. All of Vincam's customers have Carlos' personal telephone number; yet they rarely use it, because everyone in the organization takes good care of each customer.

Teresa's plan for growth at McBride is based on customer service of the highest caliber. In a 1999 national survey of information systems companies, McBride was ranked first in two of seven areas: customer service and product quality. From the beginning, Teresa's company focused all its efforts on customers. First, she chose the computer industry because she understood those customers best. Then she built her company around the processes that support her customers. Most interesting, McBride selects customers carefully, preferring those to whom her company can provide high-quality service. Finally, Teresa bases her growth estimates on the best estimates of what her customers and sales can support.

Anna's niche-market customers require quick service, prompt delivery and an experienced construction staff. Her customers are generally large construction companies that project material and staffing months in advance. In an industry where a company's word is its bond and where women are not expected to last, Anna has made a name for herself as a dependable, organized and savvy businesswoman:

> My competitive advantage right now is that I do what I say I'm going to do, that I deliver. That is very important to me. I do not try to mislead people in any way. I'm very up-front. That is why many times I will get the job, even when I'm not the low bidder.

Nancy believes she has grown because she provides twice the service her customers expect. She is competing for increasingly tight government dollars and is experiencing growth. This is a testament to great customer service. Nancy comments:

> We set objectives with each customer. Then we plan to give that customer twice as much. We have to be innovative to compete, and we do that by saving customers money. You don't just do enough to get by. You do more. The better the quality of service, the harder that customer will work to keep from losing you. We have found that even in the governmental downsizing environment, we've grown. Even as others are losing ground, we've been growing.

Communication

The unique way in which these entrepreneurs communicate and the frequency with which they communicate are important parts of their success as leaders and businesspeople. Communication in their companies is active and honest, taking many different forms, including regularly scheduled meetings, annual all-company events, informal chats and e-mail. The use of technology to communicate with employees is important for entrepreneurs in those industries where travel is essential or employees are not near the home office, but even these entrepreneurs try to make their communications personal whenever they can.

Each has a unique style of communication and uses it to paint mental pictures about the organization's vision, expectations and goals. The entrepreneurs use metaphors, anecdotes and stories, or they characterize their organizations as taking the high road. They have a tremendous amount of pride in their organizations, and it is clearly communicated. The folklore of CEO decisions and what the organization stands for is also a part of the internal communication, both formal and informal.

Tom uses anecdotes from this childhood in the south Bronx to help people understand messages about leadership and responsibility. He personally conducts the new employee briefings, which he often starts by saying, "Let me tell you why I started this company." The message is clear. He started the company to provide a supportive environment so creative minds could work together to provide the highest caliber of solutions to customers requiring the best in high-tech services. Tom also uses e-mail to conduct employee satisfaction surveys and communicates personally with employees in the field.

Teresa holds monthly meetings that all employees are asked to attend. Those on travel assignments can dial in. Annual technical training seminars are used to update employees about the status of the organization and future prospects.

Nancy regularly schedules informal meetings, "We have what we call chip-and-chats. When somebody finds a good book to read, we schedule a brown bag lunch to discuss it." But she relies heavily on what she calls her Sheet of Music:

Communicating in a time of rapid change is important and very tricky because time is so scarce. Yet, miscommunications can have dire effects. The Sheet of Music, the organizational goals and development sheet that is tailored for each employee, from my perspective makes sure that everyone is familiar with the company's goals. In addition, it makes sure that everyone's personal goals are tied to the organizational goals and that everyone understands the vision. The Sheet of Music has prevented miscommunication and sure has improved the situation around here.

The challenge to a seasoned company experiencing accelerated growth is to keep the vision fresh and clear. It is the responsibility of the CEO to communicate the vision. Carlos comments, "I think that the role of the CEO is to keep the vision, to keep a vision of what this organization will be like five or 10 years from now. People in the trenches, in the day-to-day activity, often have a hard time doing that. So, my job is to keep that in front of everybody and make sure that we keep moving in that direction."

Culture

These six entrepreneurs used a number of strategies to create their organizations. These included hiring high-potential and talented individuals and bringing them together as a team, communicating a vision and the goals to coalesce the team, and then getting them to pull in the same direction – "sing from the same page," as Nancy says. Employee ownership through stock options and ESOPs further motivated and rewarded performance and teaming. Communicating constantly, visually and personally also contributes to the sense of an organizational team. The combination of all of these, framed with the basic values and beliefs of each of the entrepreneurs, forms their unique cultures. Ultimately, the culture gives them their competitive advantage.

Carlos explains this well:

The culture has been very important to us. In fact, from our very beginning we were very keen and very obsessive, if you wish, about the establishment of the right culture. We believe that culture is set by the CEO and sort of emanates down, and both my partner and I were very much in agreement that we needed to do this, to have what I felt was to be a successful company. So, from day one, we created a culture that sort of hinged on a few important things.

First among them, according to Carlos, is a set of values. "We're a value-driven company. We articulated our values to our employees from the very beginning."

Thus, growth entrepreneurs promote strong cultures based on their values. They do it as an expression of who they are, and by doing so they guarantee that their customers will be held in high regard. The organizational culture supports employees as they provide services and products to customers. This intangible aspect of the business is what these entrepreneurs believe gives them a formidable edge. It is also what gives the organization a sense of being a team.

Growing

A penchant for growth defines successful entrepreneurs more than anything else, and is therefore a core competency. It differentiates small business owners from entrepreneurs.[1] Growth also differentiates the intrapreneur, a corporate executive who runs his or her business in an entrepreneurial manner, from other corporate leaders.

Growth is important because it translates into jobs and wealth. That, in turn, leads to community growth and revitalization, and is especially important for city leaders looking for economic solutions for neighborhoods at risk. Hence, investing in high-growth ventures can bring prosperity to areas in need of a booster shot.

The problem is identifying those start-up firms that will become fast-growth firms and those entrepreneurs who will be successful in starting and growing such firms. The magic formula has not yet been identified and is not the purpose of this book, but it is noteworthy that each of these six entrepreneurs has a special interest in growth. For all of them, the process of growth is challenging and enjoyable. They plan for it, they work through its complexities and they expect it.

When Tom outgrew his position at NASA, his vision led him to build a company that would support the growth of minds and of creativity. There was never any doubt in his mind that his would be a high-growth company, "I am going to go big. There's no other way to go. It's like the fourth law of thermodynamics. It says you can't stay static. You either shrink or grow. The market is growing. Everything around you is growing, and if you don't grow with it, then it means you're shrinking." But it won't stop there. Angel investing is another avenue for Tom as he seeks to satisfy his desire for growth. His next step is to go public.

Teresa points that it is important to enjoy the growth process, "As the organization grows, the level of complexity grows, and the amount of work grows. You have to have great people in your organization to be able to manage that growth effectively. And it is hard work. However, if you enjoy it and you like the challenge and you thrive on it, then you can do well." Teresa, like most high-growth entrepreneurs, prospers on change. They like the pace, the challenge and the mental and physical demands. "I like what I do. I enjoy the challenge. I look forward to what's next."

And if the business cannot grow as they would like and expect, entrepreneurs seek growth elsewhere. Anna is a good example. She had been steadily building her construction business. But after she "resized" to take advantage of a niche that provided large margins in a small-margin, high-volume industry, she looked for growth through acquisition and as an angel investor.

Entrepreneurs who want a fast-growing company seem to have a radar that attracts them to opportunities in fast-growing markets. In such cases, opportunities that appear merely good are dismissed in favor of opportunities that yield the most growth.

For these six entrepreneurs, this was a visceral process. Carlos and his partner sought several opportunities in food and in low-tech business. But what caught their imagination, what cemented their commitment, against the advice of experts, was an opportunity that meant growing an industry, not just a business. Certainly, the initial growth of their business was slow, but the ultimate vision had the telltale signs of tremendous growth potential. Carlos and his partner had that "gut feeling" on that Saturday morning, napkin and pen at hand.

All six entrepreneurs used those same words to describe that feeling of recognizing the opportunity. Danny had it about Spanish-language television, Nancy about moving her company to a distant region. She called it "gut and go." Similarly, Anna recalls getting that feeling two years after she started her business, the point at which she felt she became an entrepreneur.

Teresa had that gut feeling when she realized the potential of her first computer as a tool for business management. Tom sensed it when he was moved to start a high-tech business that would solve problems for customers by providing the right work environment for scientists and problem-solvers. That gut feeling may be the ability to recognize what feels comfortable, that combination of stuff that has the makings of growth – scale, complexity and significance.

Most of these entrepreneurs went quickly from gut to plan. They planned their growth. It was not a chance event – certainly not a surprise. Carlos and his partner quickly went from napkin to plan. They even had their plan reviewed by colleagues and friends.

Teresa planned the growth at McBride from the very beginning with her first-year goals. Though the process has changed and improved, her planning continues. She determined at the start how much growth she wanted, how much she could fund and how much the infrastructure of the company could sustain. Then she negotiated funding and grew into her plan. For two years she purposely slowed down to work on her company's infrastructure before continuing the growth she wanted. She still managed to grow by about $5 million during the slowdown, and the next year she made up for that slower growth.

These entrepreneurs are attracted to growth with a purpose. The winning package for them is to build something significant. Danny's ever-increasing circle of influence started early with his family's strong tradition of service. Service to others on a large scale is a big part of Danny's vision. He does not know where that need for grandness came from, but he recognized early that the community's needs were large.

Playing NFL football, doing community service in schools, managing radio and television stations and buying, turning around and selling media companies while supporting the growth of Spanish-language media – a growth industry in the United States – are all examples of his continuing love affair with purposeful growth. As a venture capital investor, he currently nurtures the formation of high-potential companies in order to support their growth and reap the benefits. The result has been to spotlight a minority success in the venture capital industry, an area where minorities are just now beginning to participate successfully. His next area of concentration is to form a team – his SWAT team – to support the growth of inner-city businesses.

Successful growth requires discipline. Carlos remembers:

We grew slowly at first. We were very disciplined. We reinvested heavily in the business and we were very careful about how much money we took out of the business. Basically, we took out as little as possible. We were very careful not to mix personal expenses with business expenses. But most of all, we were disciplined because that is the kind of business we wanted. We wanted it to reflect our values about ethics in business.

For Carlos, industry image meant that he had to help grow the industry, position himself to affect legislation that would promote the legitimacy of his industry, and ward off unethical players. He and his partner became founding members of what was then called the National Staff Leasing Association, the industry trade association. Carlos recalls:

Right after legislation passed in Florida, the industry began to grow. 1991 was a watershed year. We had grown substantially. By then we had probably about 20 or 30 employees, internally. We were growing fast. Then we opened an operation in Michigan with a local partner. This was our first venture outside Florida. In 1992, Hurricane

Andrew hit Florida; that was then we realized that our expansion had paid off. In fact, we didn't miss any of our payrolls. In 1993, we continued to grow and had to move out of our original location into a new building, a huge building for us at the time.

These entrepreneurs love the challenge, the process and the rewards of building something of significance. Nancy captures her personal growth experience well: "I like creativity and leadership and vision and moving forward. It's a great, wonderful thing to grow out of a cocoon and into a butterfly. And I think all people can do that."

Learning

The penchant for business growth is closely related to an attraction to lifelong learning and personal growth. Lifelong learning requires actively seeking relevant information and quickly acquiring the skills necessary to manage the complexities of growth. It also requires readily abandoning tried-and-true behaviors that are no longer adaptive.

For entrepreneurs, this habit of lifelong learning extends to knowing themselves, their business, their industry and how to manage risk. And since each of these factors changes at different rates, learning never stops for fast-growth entrepreneurs.

Teresa goes out of her way to visit other businesses and schedules business tours as often as she can, taking copious notes:

I am always looking for new information, new strategies, new ways of looking at old business practices. I will never know everything. I sometimes run into people who are absolutely correct – they know they know it all. An entrepreneur would find it difficult to stay in business with that attitude.

Likewise, Nancy believes that she must stay abreast of all major developments in business and her high-tech industry.

"I'm a quick study. I can read. I can be a sponge. I look at people who have been successful and I try to emulate what they do. Perhaps since I wasn't able to finish my formal education, I have been willing to watch and study successful people. It is important to be open to ideas."

Danny has entered enough fields that he has a well-established process of learning about an industry to see how he can add value. He has overcome his weaknesses through hard work: for instance, learning to speak commercial Spanish, literally in front of thousands of people who were none too shy to offer criticism.

Know Thyself

Donald Sexton,[2] author and editor of books on entrepreneurship, quotes Socrates to his students: "To thy self be true." The process of entrepreneurship requires that the entrepreneurs know themselves – their strengths and weaknesses – very well.

The six entrepreneurs featured here have this characteristic in common. A clear knowledge of their own interests, goals and values has enabled them to build strategies that worked. They can anticipate personal issues and training needs. Most significantly, they make the most of their talents and unique circumstances.

Self-assessment seems to occur continuously for these entrepreneurs, and as illustrated in the interviews, turning points have come about after deliberate self-assessment. Danny took stock of his weaknesses first, then his strengths. He did this every time he entered a new pursuit – when he decided to pursue football rather than basketball in high school, when he went into Spanish-language television knowing his Spanish was weak. But he knew from experience that he could work to overcome his weaknesses. Similarly, when he entered venture capital, he knew that financial modeling was not his strength; instead, his experience in business growth and the contacts he had developed would be essential.

Nancy used what she calls her "life board of directors" to help with self-assessment. These are close friends and colleagues whom she trusts to give her honest feedback. She seeks their ideas on options and potential opportunities, as well as perceptions about her strengths and weaknesses. The board members she values the most are those who challenge her positions, preferences and strengths while suggesting how to deal with her weaknesses.

An important role of partners is to help with self-assessment. Anna's first partner played a definite role in influencing her to start a business. His strong opinion was based on his assessment of her strengths compared with other vendors with whom he worked. This caused Anna to evaluate herself and her options for business ownership. But then Anna had always evaluated her strengths against others. This is what caused her to be such a successful student and a successful businesswoman in an industry where women are rare.

Carlos had a long-time associate as a partner. Their daily exchange of ideas and opinions was a way for them to evaluate themselves and their business prospects and later to evaluate their progress in growing the business and the industry.

Music may have been Tom's self-assessment tool. The discipline of comparing his talent against those of talented musicians and later talented scientists helped him understand his strengths and weaknesses. He continues to evaluate his performance by reading and participating in executive leadership development programs.

Another skill the six entrepreneurs share is promoting personal growth as a part of leading a fast-growth firm. These entrepreneurs assimilate change quickly, which may be a determining factor in managing a fast-growth firm. For example, when Anna was faced with the problem of workers using drugs on the work site, she did a double-take. But her decision for managing the crisis was already made.

Fast growth challenges values and interpersonal relationships. Growth sometimes means leaving partners or key staff behind when the organization outgrows their style, talent or contributions. Tom originally had a partner who was also a friend. As the organization grew more structured, the partner's informal style became a significant concern. Eventually, Tom offered the partner a retirement package, which he accepted. But the discomfort and subsequent delay in getting this done exemplify the difficulties and the interpersonal challenges involved in continued fast growth. Tom acknowledges that he should have acted sooner, but he knew himself well enough to recognize that his personal values regarding friendship superseded the need to grow.

Change is stressful, so knowing how to manage the emotional costs of growth is important. Danny retreats to Calexico when he needs a break from putting together investment deals. Teresa takes regularly scheduled vacations and finds that it makes her a better leader. Tom finds respite in developing new ways to communicate and support the growth of his leadership team. This is a great source of pride. Carlos derives refreshment from supporting and bringing together community leaders to promote ethical government.

As part of their self-awareness, these fast-growth entrepreneurs also know that their personal concerns regarding power and control can get in the way of supporting growth. Entrepreneurs interested in fast growth must learn to delegate. Hence, the six quickly found talented people and figured out the process of delegating effectively, which included putting controls in place and developing procedures for monitoring them. The six have partners or management teams that enable them to concentrate on growth activities instead of focusing on day-to-day operations. Carlos, Anna and Danny started with partners. Tom, Nancy and Teresa have management teams. All have measures and standards that keep track of growth as it happens.

A related growth issue involves relinquishing enough control to let investors assume an interest in the company as a way of funding growth. For entrepreneurs, a smaller part of a bigger and stronger organization is better than a larger proportion of a smaller organization. As a result, these fast-growth entrepreneurs all sought funding for growth, whether through venture capital, financial organizations, IPOs or mergers.

After going public, Carlos and his partner merged with a larger organization – a tough decision, given their significant investment in Vincam, but par for the course for them. Tom's future IPO will bring expansion at the expense of control, but he is looking forward to that.

Decisions and strategies differ because each entrepreneur has a unique set of talents, strengths and weaknesses; but they know themselves and their personal requirements for growth well, and these skills have been essential for the growth of their businesses.

Know Thy Business

For the six entrepreneurs, growth meant learning entirely new industries or expanding their knowledge as their industries evolved and customers changed. Knowing the mechanics of a business – financial statements, measures of successful, organizational performance, customer groups, vendors, and community constituencies – is essential. While it may seem obvious that being successful requires knowledge of the business, these entrepreneurs knew their businesses so well that they could predict how any particular change would affect the organization and its growth potential. This advantage allowed them to move quickly and to compete effectively against corporations much larger than theirs.

Knowing the numbers from the very beginning – what they mean and how to read any deviations in performance standards – was a basic skill for each of these entrepreneurs.

Each spent a considerable amount of time understanding the mechanics of the business. This gave them confidence to negotiate, manage risks and lead their organizations, as well as to select options and manage performance.

Teresa's and Nancy's emphasis on benchmarking – knowing the business from the very beginning – are great examples of how they built combinations that led to success. They spent considerable time and resources studying how companies grow – what worked and what did not. Further, their benchmarking never stops. It is an essential part of their role within the organization.

Teresa also understood the importance of ongoing technical training and communication in her fast-changing industry. Though McBride sells computer hardware, services keep her in front of her customers. As policy, she focuses on customers and technical situations that she knows are well within the capability of her organization. This means knowing her industry and her business well. The reward for this kind of diligence is consistently high customer service ratings in national surveys, where she is compared with organizations much larger than hers.

Tom emphasized the importance of developing leadership within his organization. In a high-tech firm, micromanaging slows growth. Individual leadership is essential. Hence, Tom spends a considerable amount of effort to ensure that leadership development is ongoing.

Anna figured out her specialty within the construction industry – the niche in which she competes most successfully. She thoughtfully manages her strengths of dependability and expertise to outbid competitors. That way, she has developed access points to choice projects.

The explosive growth of Spanish-language television was due in part to unmet demand, but the technology Danny and his partners chose was consistently ahead of the largest and most successful commercial television giants, ABC and NBC. The use of the latest technology allowed Danny's company to offer high-quality and innovative televised services at the only price they could afford – since the cost of commercial technology was prohibitive. But first they had to understand the technology and how it would work for their purposes.

Carlos and Danny are helpful examples of understanding the industries they were helping to build – the laws, the competition and public perception. Carlos knew that the business opportunity was there, despite the reasons given him for not pursuing it. Danny is a master at figuring out industries, the reason he has been so successful as a venture capital investor.

Knowing the business and the industry has allowed these entrepreneurs to continue their steep growth trends. While it may seem intuitive that knowledge of the business is essential to be successful, the changing business environment and the accelerated growth process mean that knowledge of a business or industry is ever-changing. Hence, lifelong learning is essential.

Know Thy Risk

Like growth, taking calculated risk often differentiates entrepreneurs from other businesspeople. These entrepreneurs know how to manage risk. They do not simply take risks or "play the odds." Anna said it best, "I may go out on a limb, but I make sure it is a very strong limb." Knowing how to manage risk means analyzing the risk, studying options and determining what is needed to minimize and control the risk. By the time entrepreneurs take the risk, the course has been planned and plotted, with strong contingency plans in the wings. Few surprises should arise; but if they do, the entrepreneurs immediately assess their potential for risk and take action.

Carlos and his partner developed their business plan to assess risk and figure out how to manage it. When their expert advisors counseled against pursuing the plan, they knew their decision to continue was risky. But their analysis led them to believe that the risk was reasonable, temporary and assumable. They later became involved with the National Association of Leased Employees and actively sought legislative action as a way of managing and minimizing their risks, so they could grow their business to its potential.

Similarly, leaving a good position with NASA was risky for Tom, but he understood exactly how he would make it work. Since he had established his base prior to leaving NASA, the risk lay in building his own organization. He felt he could manage this risk by hiring the best talent available.

Danny's decision to leave football was balanced by his personal conviction that hard work would pay off. It was no casual conviction – Danny had already seen that hard work leads to success. He knew he could manage the risk involved. He then left Spanish-language television to become a venture capital investor, knowing that in this new industry, his willingness to work hard would enable him to manage the risk involved.

Teaming

If the stereotype of entrepreneurs is that they are loners, then these entrepreneurs do not fit the bill. They are members of many teams. In some they lead, in others they participate as members. Each has his or her own style and interest in engaging teams, and they all understand that their success is in large part based on how well they are able to create, contribute to or grow their teams.

The Organizational Team

Creating a team within the growing organization represents a shift from a start-up to a fully functioning organization. One of the challenges of fast-growth entrepreneurs is to instill that entrepreneurial drive and spirit for growth within their organizations. The entrepreneurs featured here use a number of strategies to promote entrepreneurial spirit and teamwork. These include hiring the most talented individuals and then building teams; sharing company ownership and success through stock options and ESOPs; creating unique styles of communication to set a clear vision, expectations and goals; and promoting cultures based on their values through strong leadership.

Hiring, Then Teaming

For Tom, hiring is equivalent to scouting talent for an all-star winning team. He goes for the best players and then uses all his abilities and skills to make them into that winning team:

> The one law that I learned is to always hire better than you. If you learn that law, believe it and really live it – which is always very hard – it pays off. The shame of doing otherwise is that the lowest rung of the ladder is always the least competent, because everyone down the line is doing likewise. The result is a team with poor players.

A leadership group that is not a team can cost the company dearly, especially in growth. Don Sexton provides an example from his own experience, "When each function is charged with growth, marketing naturally seeks to sell a wide range of products and services, while manufacturing seeks long manufacturing runs to minimize cost of production. When this happens, the company is literally working against itself."[3]

Employee Ownership and Partnership

Employee ownership seems to resolve the one issue that entrepreneurs feel stifles organizational growth – that employees do not share their sense of urgency to support the growth of the organization. Giving employees ownership transforms them into partners. Tom's company offers both stock options and an ESOP. Tom remarks:

> I believe in employee ownership. We are an employee-owned company today. We have stock options. So we have hundreds of employees who are owners. Plus, with our ESOP, all of our employees are owners. Since I believe in ownership, I also believe that people who own things should be responsible for taking care of them; so I take great pains to get people involved in the decision process. In the early days that helped shape the culture, the policies and the processes we used to manage. Perhaps to a lesser extent today, that's still the way we operate.

Nancy also offers stock ownership and an ESOP but feels that the culture plays an important part in making employees feel they are a part of a stable and humane company:

> We're also an employee stock ownership company. I have an ESOP so people will have a vested interest in the company. Everyone who participates in the retirement plan participates in ownership of the company. We also have a very aggressive incentive stock option plan, so employees who are the superstars have an additional opportunity to become owners.

Though very unusual in the construction industry, Anna's company has a profit-sharing plan for her core staff. "There are about 21 people in the plan. It's non-contributory. It was set up as a pension plan accessible after age 65."

The Vendor Team

These high-growth entrepreneurs feel that vendors are an important part of their organizational team – a noteworthy concept, since the growth potential of the firm represents growth opportunity for the vendor as well.

Teresa does not simply negotiate the best terms for financing her growth; she incorporates her vendors into the business process. She comments:

> When I was seeking more flexible funding, finance companies would tell me that there are industry standards for loans to companies in my industry. I would respond that I needed them to be our partner and that I could not survive in business over the long term if, for this amount of risk they would get this percentage of profitability. I would suggest that they should not lend me money if I was that irresponsible. They would often agree with me.

Anna found it hard to get insurance initially because she did not have a track record, but she finally found an agent who trusted her. She has kept this insurance company even though others are now clamoring for her business. She considers her agent a member of her team:

> When I first tried to get insurance, nobody would give it to me. I had no track record and they wouldn't insure start-ups. … Eventually, I found an agent that, for whatever reason, believed in me. I was still operating out of my house. To this day, he's my agent. Right now he gets first refusal of my business. I can get 10 people who want my business now.

Business, Industry and Professional Teams

Among the many important teams of which they are members, the six entrepreneurs are careful to take time to participate in business, industry and professional associations. These groups serve many purposes. Initially, they are a source of learning opportunities and networking that most entrepreneurs seek. As they gain experience and their companies achieve high growth, the entrepreneurs' roles within these organizations change to those of senior contributors and mentors to other entrepreneurs. Entrepreneurs value these expert teams greatly.

The Hispanic Chamber of Commerce is an excellent venue for networking and plays an important role on entrepreneurial teams in the early stages of many companies' growth. Both Anna and Nancy have found their chamber memberships extremely valuable. As Anna points out, "There are members of the chamber who are in my situation who are not my competitors ... I have a very good network and I have never been shy about asking. I might even ask an opinion of competitors that work on the projects that we don't work."

Tom finds value in his memberships in professional associations, and Carlos, Danny and Teresa are active in their industry associations. Entrepreneurs' memberships in professional associations and organizations extend benefits to the community at large and enable entrepreneurs to share their talents with those who need help.

Summary

Leadership for these six entrepreneurs is about setting a clear vision, establishing ethical customer service as a permanent goal, and communicating this clearly and frequently and cementing a culture that supports their personal values. They value and enjoy growth and do so by subscribing to lifelong personal growth, fully understanding their business and industry and seeking to develop teams – their organizational teams, their vendor teams as well as industry and association teams. These leadership best practices come together to create the entrepreneurs' fast-growth companies.

Notes

---

[1]Donald L. Sexton and N. Bowman-Upton, *Entrepreneurship: Creativity and Growth* (New York: Mcmillian Publishing Company, 1991)

[2]Donald L. Sexton, *To thy self be true*, Personal communication (2000) April, 3.

[3]Sexton, *Teamwork in manufacturing*. Personal communication (2000) April, 3.

CHAPTER ELEVEN

THE LEGACY CYCLE

There are many roads to entrepreneurship and to success. Whether a person has an early start or a later start, business ownership seems to depend on life choices. Yet the influence of adults – parents, guardians and mentors – is paramount in instilling values and shaping development and, as illustrated here, played an important role in the success of these entrepreneurs. They used their childhood experiences, whether nurturing or difficult, to create a successful life. And the value adults placed on them as children, by being present and available, guided the children's talents toward success. From receiving this personal legacy from the adults in their lives, they have gone on to give to others, especially to children. Among those children are tomorrow's leaders, who in turn will keep the legacy of receiving and giving alive.

Receiving

From the personal accounts related in this book, it is easy to see that childhood experiences had a tremendous effect on the choices these six made, and that the adults in their lives –

parents, grandparents, mentors and community leaders – were the catalysts that helped form values and mold development. It is logical to assume that somehow the process leading to entrepreneurial success begins early in life.

Being born into a family that owns a business or that has a tradition of entrepreneurship, as in Teresa McBride's situation, provides an early education in many practical areas. Teresa's day-to-day contribution to the family restaurant was on-the-job training for later development of supervisory skills, the mechanics of running a business and, most valuable, the importance of respecting people and their differences. This is the benchmark that characterizes the culture she nurtures in her company today and strongly believes gives her a competitive advantage.

Teresa's family worked in large scale. Her father told her stories that opened the world to her, so that she became comfortable with grand scale even as a teenager. She recalls that when her friends wanted to have a small party she could not help but organize a grand fiesta. Picnics became community events. Her grandmother's house was open every day to anyone who needed a meal. Her grandfather participated in the community as sheriff, as owner of the restaurant and the gas station and as the town's informal banker. The McBrides saw possibilities everywhere.

Carlos Saladrigas also observed family business ownership as a child, recalling the creativity with which his mother ran her business. His survival instincts and knack for turning difficult situations into opportunities developed early. This natural inclination became a set of highly adaptive behaviors that helped him lead a successful business within a budding and fast-growing industry. Carlos managed the added complications of poor public perception, customer wariness and outdated government regulations with aplomb, recognizing them as opportunities and relishing their complexities.

He might have applied his many skills to several areas, but a persistent mentor urged Carlos to pursue a graduate degree at Harvard. This proved to be a turning point in his career and his life. That MBA made him an attractive job candidate and valuable employee at PepsiCo. Later, when the desire to change his lifestyle caused him to consider entrepreneurial options, he was well equipped to see opportunities in the professional employee organization industry and to follow his instincts in spite of the advice of trusted expert colleagues who advised against such a business.

Danny Villanueva's family dedicated themselves to community service, not entrepreneurship, but his mother recognized that her ninth child had a gift for influence and leadership. It was a source of both pride and worry to her as she set out to shape his attitudes about what was really important. The desire for service influenced Danny's decision to move to Spanish-language television from football. It was a desire to influence large numbers of people, but the entrepreneurial side that emerged from this decision was perhaps a welcome surprise.

Anna Cablik's decision to become a business owner and to grow through acquisitions resulted from an analysis of her options. Business ownership proved to be the best option, followed by growth through acquisition. While self-confidence and determination played an important role in Anna's success, she became an entrepreneur largely as a result of her adult experiences and decisions. Yet, she became comfortable with risk early crossing swollen rivers on her way to school. Further, her parents expected academic excellence and practical common sense.

Tom Velez's father used examples from the immediate environment to teach valuable lessons about ethics and proper conduct, and he showed his son a way out of a precarious environment. These are the lessons Tom now incorporates into the culture of his firm through anecdotes about leadership lessons from the South Bronx. Tom recalls times when he could have taken an easier, more tempting route, but out of respect for his father he selected the high road. The discipline he developed through his music studies influenced his success, but it was his experience as an orchestra conductor – the scale and the leadership – that inspired him the most.

Nancy Archuleta's childhood experiences prompted in her a determination to overcome challenges. She was born with the heart to survive. It is difficult to find experiences in her childhood that would have promoted an interest in business ownership and less so in high-growth business. But she willed her way into entrepreneurship, just as she had willed her way out of a desperate and debilitating marriage. If anything, her difficult childhood kindled in her the ability to dream and to envision a better future, and to recognize that she would have to make it happen herself.

Fortunately, she had the spiritual strength and the support of caring teachers and mentors. "I'm not here because I'm a product of myself. I'm a product of what the Good Lord has made and what people a lot smarter than me have made. I'm a product of the role models that I've had. I remind myself of that every day when I look in the mirror."

Giving

Successful Hispanic entrepreneurs are role models who build communities. Through their leadership in their communities they prove the importance of education, hard work, philanthropy and community service. The jobs they generate help families create wealth. They help build community infrastructures and, through their involvement in and contribution to the political process, they promote community power bases. They do this first and foremost by example. Their success as business owners and entrepreneurs puts them in a position of power to influence others. Second, their active involvement in community activities makes them available and visible to youngsters as they mature and consider future options.

Aida Alvarez, the head of the Small Business Administration calls Hispanic entrepreneurs "unsung heroes" because, quietly and steadily, they give back to their communities. They realized early on the relationship between business success and community growth. But most of all, they wanted to pay back a debt to parents, mentors and teachers for having taken the time and interest to encourage, inspire and urge them along.

These six entrepreneurs are active in their communities as leaders and as investors. Their philanthropic activities set them apart as remarkable individuals. At first glance, philanthropy is not often tied to entrepreneurial activity. Yet, entrepreneurs have founded many philanthropic organizations. Therefore, supporting entrepreneurial growth today may also mean supporting the growth of nonprofit organizations tomorrow. In communities of need, this is essential.

Several things stand out. First, while all the entrepreneurs were proud of the programs they led and supported, they did not like taking credit for the time and resources they invested. Second, growth – a natural part of doing business for them – was blended into their community service. As participants, they very naturally made suggestions and recommendations toward growth. Third, those who founded their own nonprofit organizations to encourage community development now are involved in start-up and growing organizations in other areas. Fourth, there was a genuine interest in giving. If there was a business advantage to participating in philanthropic activities, it was considered a bonus and not part of the process of giving back. The entrepreneurs gave in appreciation for what they had received as children or young adults, simply because it was the right thing to do.

Destino 2000

Continuing his family's tradition of community service, Danny Villanueva is involved in all aspects of his community, from voter registration, the arts and children's programs to Boy Scouts and child and adult literacy programs. But special mention has to go to Danny's *Destino* 2000 (Destiny 2000), a program of the Ventura Community Foundation. He is personally leading one of three funds, the Latino Initiative. This community support effort has a goal of $200,000 by end of the year 2000 when the fund closes. This is an entrepreneurial model of philanthropy. It involves Hispanic families in the process of fund building and distribution, and sets up the fund to be self-contained. Each charter family donates $1,000 and has two years to honor its pledge to continue as a founding member. The funds are invested and the families distribute the annual interest to fund community organizations.

There is no doubt that this effort will be successful, given Danny's commitment. However, to make sure, Danny built in safeguards. The Irvine Foundation gave the initial $25,000 to begin building interest on the investment that first year. Other foundations and corporations contributed small first-year grants to help build momentum. The Destino 2000 families used a portion of those grants the first year to begin the process of distribution.

The personal and inspirational aspect of this program must be emphasized. Awareness meetings were held in family homes and in small restaurants. Danny calls this the Tupperware-party approach. But they were much more; they were legacy meetings. Many families gave in memory of their parents and grandparents, who had dedicated their lives to the education and well-being of their children. Now, their adult children were in a position to continue and expand the cycle

As of October 1999, the first round of meetings yielded $157,000 in Ventura County alone. Those funds were invested conservatively. At the end of the year, Danny staged two events for donors and recipients. The first was a reunion held to thank all participating families. About 75 to 100 families attended. Several days later at a luncheon hosted by a local bank, the nominating committee distributed the first funds to community organizations. As part of their acceptance speeches, the receiving organizations were asked to mention how they were going to use the funds.

The Ventura Community Foundation is considering using this entrepreneurial model to start a cornerstone fund. Like the other Destino 2000 funds, donations will be invested and the interest used to cover the foundation's overhead expenses in perpetuity.

College Bound

Teresa created the McBride Foundation in 1994 to address the high dropout rate of disadvantaged children. The foundation supports a flagship program called College Bound. In Teresa's unique and creative way of living her values, she has devised a program that cannot help but meet its goals of helping more disadvantaged children to attend college. It works like this: A college or vocational school student forms a pact with an elementary school class, usually from a Title 1 school. That student agrees to visit the school six times during the year to provide an inside view of their student life. This includes sharing difficulties he or she encounters and sharing report card and test grades with the class.

In so doing, the children become the advisory board to that college or vocational school student, providing suggestions and asking no-nonsense questions. Teresa recalls a college student who was reluctant to discuss his grade on a particular exam; the advisory board marched the college student to the principal's office and called his college professor. The professor, amused, and with the permission of his student, provided the information.

At the end of the school year, the college student takes the children on a college tour to make real all the information and stories the children have heard during the year. The results have been phenomenal. In a pre-program survey of fourth- and fifth-grade children, 47 percent had already planned to drop out of high school. An exit survey showed that all but 7 percent now planned to graduate. When parents were invited to participate in the program, 70 percent of the parents attended all six sessions.

Perhaps most telling of the powerful nature of these programs are the McBride Foundation mottos – "Helping Children Help Themselves" and "Learning is a Lifelong Journey."

Ethical Government

Carlos Saladrigas is involved in countless corporate and college boards as well as community development and health organizations. He strongly believes that business success supports the development of community.

Carlos comments:

Giving back means a lot to me. I came out of my Jesuit education with what I think is a very clear purpose in life. I have a very significant, affirmative duty to maximize the gifts that I've been given, whatever those gifts and skills are. I have been charged to do the best I can, to work as hard as I can for the betterment of the world around us. That has been my guiding light all along in terms of what we need to do. I consider staying in business and creating jobs as giving back, too. It is a big piece of what I need to do. I take that responsibility pretty seriously.

One vision and mission is so heartfelt that hearing him speak about it is an immediate inspiration. This effort is a vital manifestation of Carlos' value system as a parent, a community member, a business owner and an advocate for democracy: "At the end of the day, we live here. Our children live here, and we cannot afford to see this community continue to go down the path it was going. Corruption destroys absolutely, totally, our trust in government. We cannot afford to sit back and idly watch our community go down that road."

In 1998, Carlos spearheaded an effort against official corruption in Dade County, Florida. The *Mesa Redonda* (The Round Table), a Hispanic community development group that Carlos helped found, organized the Miami/Dade Alliance for Ethical Government.[1] This organization, composed of prominent community leaders in religion, government, education and business, is a community effort intent on curbing corruption in Miami.

The Miami/Dade Alliance for Ethical Government is a 501(C) (3) nonprofit group presided over by Gerald Hogan, retired chief justice of the Supreme Court of Florida. The Alliance has 125 trustees, a board of directors and an executive committee. Its purpose is to make systemic changes in government to address corruption in Dade County, and it hopes to accomplish this in three years.

The Alliance is fundamentally a think tank. The official outcome will be a series of strategies and recommendations to the city government of Miami. On a more practical level, the Alliance hopes to inspire all business owners, government officials, religious leaders and educators to act ethically. Just as corrupt officials are well known to those interested in influencing government, so too would this group of leaders be known for the opposite attribute – their ethical conduct. Once they achieve the critical membership, they hope to turn the tide of habitual corrupt behavior in Miami/Dade County. Information and social policy formation is their goal, so they discuss all areas where corruption would have an easy entry: government procurement practices, lobbying, the election process and finance reform, official term limits, political parties and their role, and compensation of elected officials. At last count, the group had raised $240,000. It has a goal of $300,000 for each of the next three years.

Entrepreneurship and Community Development

Anna Cablik does not like to showcase the substantial contributions she makes to her community. In Anna's mind, community development is very important:

If my community looks good, I look good. I'm very blessed. Where I came from, I had nothing. If I can inspire somebody else to get where I am, then there will be two of us. I am very involved, and I see it as my duty to help people who might not be as fortunate as I am. Giving back is the morally right thing to do.

Anna gives a percentage of her revenue to the organizations she helps support. She has done this even in the two years when her company did not make a profit, because she feels it is her responsibility. But of all her community development work, Anna is most active and committed to business development. She feels that when people start and grow successful businesses, everyone benefits. That is why she is so active in the Hispanic Chamber of Commerce, both in Atlanta and at the national level, where she is on the board of directors, "To me, what businesspeople can give to the community is their leadership as role models for future entrepreneurs."

Hispanic role models are very important to Anna:

I am a private person who does not like publicity. But I am very conscious that the Hispanic community needs positive role models, especially here in Atlanta. I feel that the people who are highlighted in the papers and magazines are not what I would consider very good role models.

When I became the chair of the Atlanta Hispanic Chamber of Commerce in 1992, I decided to make it a point to establish a healthy working relationship with the local papers, even though I am not a media person. It is a small contribution, but I am hoping that as more leaders emerge in the Hispanic community, it will all add up and make a real difference.

Community development is difficult if resources are tight, but Anna sees a slow change in the Hispanic community toward giving to local communities. "Latinos support their families, especially their families in Latin America. They also support the church, which then helps missions and orphanages. Sometimes that means that the local communities get shortchanged. But we are more affluent now and I see that changing."

Employee Involvement In Philanthropy

Nancy believes strongly in community support. This is part of her Native American tradition. The zia, the Native American symbol for the sun, is her company's logo. It reminds her staff that the basic values of life are important no matter how fast the company is growing. The belief espouses giving back double whatever you take. If you take one tree, you plant two. No matter what you do, you always leave it better than you found it. It is Nancy's philosophy, and it permeates her business.

As a result, MEVATEC employees are encouraged to work on community projects. By providing time and support through her employees, Nancy ensures that a wide variety of organizations and community needs are addressed. A percentage of the company's annual receipts are allocated for community support to help the less fortunate.

Nancy channels her philanthropic contributions through existing organizations. Among her favorites is the United

Way, because it reaches so many people. Hispanic organizations, especially college funds and educational programs, are
among other top organizations supported by MEVATEC.
Nancy's personal favorites include shelters for victims of
domestic abuse, such as Hope Place, where she serves on the
board, and the National Children's Advocacy Center.

Role Model in Science and Technology

Tom's philosophy is that as an executive and leader of an
organization, he must give to worthwhile organizations. Not
surprisingly, like his father before him, he believes in the
inherent value of a good solid education. Therefore, his personal interest is in increasing and supporting Hispanic representation in science and technology.

Hence, Tom commits himself to Hispanic schools and professional organizations such as the Society of Hispanic
Engineers and Professionals. Aside from providing summer
jobs in his company to young adults interested in seeing
what high-tech organizations do, Tom lectures on education,
technology and science. He sees a marked improvement in
the numbers of qualified Hispanic college students. He
recalled a recent lecture opportunity:

> I was standing in front of 50 or so young college graduates
> from some of the best schools in the United States – from
> Harvard, MIT and Stanford – majoring in chemical engi-
> neering, electrical engineering, computer science and
> business, and I marveled at the power in the room. Can
> you imagine all these young Hispanic women and men?
> Yes, about 30 percent or 40 percent were women. I had to
> tell them, 'If I were you, I would just get together at lunch
> and create a company right there.'

Summary

From child to child, the investment pays off. As children, these entrepreneurs reaped the benefits from adults that cared enough to give – to give their leadership, their time and their resources. It made a big difference. Today they are compelled to do likewise. And in doing so they assure that future generations will keep this legacy going, and thus promote the essential development of their communities.

All six entrepreneurs contribute to the Hispanic and mainstream communities by participating in political, social, commercial, educational and philanthropic organizations; this involvement empowers them and other Hispanics in their communities. They are influential in their communities, and others listen to them and ask for their opinions. A community's strength comes from such power; this needs to be added to the portfolio of sociopolitical efforts that communities engage in as they emerge from communities of need to communities of power.

Notes

[1]John Dorschner, *Corruption for the Love of Money*, Miami Herald Library Archive. www.herald.com/dade/archive/port/docs/0999920.htm. September 20.

CHAPTER TWELVE

¡VISIÓN!
EPILOGUE

The entrepreneurs profiled in this book have shared with us the richness of their experience. It is a gift they offered graciously and enthusiastically. Their gift is inspirational. They met challenges with courage and business smarts and succeeded where others might not. They are successful businesspeople, interested and involved in high growth. They have developed their winning combination by meshing strengths, weaknesses, skills and interests with many other personal attributes.

While their specific, unique combinations might not be right for anyone else, they do offer a number of best practices they believe contributed to their success as business founders, owners and growers. These leadership best practices provide guidance to others in critical areas of business development and growth. They allow new entrepreneurs to move faster and beyond these lessons to more advanced areas of personal and business development. Their focus on establishing and evolving their vision, their personal requirements for learning and growth; on building culture, fostering honest communication and concentrating on ethical customer practices as they built and grew their businesses points out those intangible essentials for business success.

Thus, the account of the successful practices of these Hispanic entrepreneurs is a story about business – an important story. But, the story of successful entrepreneurs who give back and, in doing so, contribute to the development of communities, is much more. Certainly, they are not the only, and may not have even been the main contributors to the development of Hispanic communities, but entrepreneurs are important contributors. The legacy these entrepreneurs leave behind as business role models and as successful leaders is perhaps second to that of their philanthropy and its effect on Hispanic communities. But most important of all is the legacy that evolves as the children who benefit from their leadership carry on the tradition of receiving and giving back.

That is why, placed within the context of the larger Hispanic community, the success of entrepreneurs is so important. They are affected by the progress the community has made and in turn affect the continued growth of the community. It is difficult to determine which came first, or which is more significant. What is important is that this almost symbiotic relationship cultivates a realistic vision of a better future. These entrepreneurs are merely six of nearly two million business owners who are steadily making progress and bringing others along as they prosper.

The wealth entrepreneurs create for themselves and the families they employ, the community infrastructure they help build, the political empowerment they generate through their involvement in the political process – the strong connection between business success and the development of their community – are what make the statistics about their growth exciting.

The nearly two million entrepreneurs, the 305 percent growth in numbers of businesses, compared to 26 percent for all businesses; and their remarkable rise in revenues – about $184 billion, a 400 percent increase since 1987 – is significant statistically and significant socially. And the timing could not be better.

The Hispanic community is poised to be the largest U.S. minority in as little as 10 years. Today Latinos are the largest minority among children. On one hand, the demographic trends look promising. As an aggregate, this growing group of 35 million has the buying power to command the attention of major corporations, the political potential to sway strategy, and the charisma to influence popular culture. By contrast, its members are also the youngest, the least educated and have the lowest income of all minority groups.

This young group will come of age about the time that baby boomers, the largest group of adults in the United States, retires. Hispanics' earning potential will directly affect the Social Security system. Their future will affect the future of many Americans, minority or otherwise.

Hispanics have a rich past, a rich present and an even richer future to look forward to. The list of Hispanic and minority "firsts" will get longer as opportunity becomes more democratized. Latinas, in particular, will keep on making their mark as business owners, in government, corporations and in nonprofit organizations.

Hispanic businesses will continue to grow in number, complexity and scope as the movement into the next level of Hispanic enterprise is led by succeeding generations of highly educated and experienced Hispanic entrepreneurs and professionals. These are the children of the vision, the children of laborers, blue-collar workers, immigrants and entrepreneurs who have worked hard, sacrificed and pooled resources so that their children could achieve more than they did. Other children – those fortunate enough to have mentors who open their eyes to possibility and opportunity – will receive support and encouragement from community leaders and organizations that will help them face the risks and understand what it means to be responsible to themselves, their families and their communities. And thus the legacy, which began with vision, should perpetuate itself and all will benefit.

¡Viva visión!

Index

¡Visión!
Hispanic Entrepreneurs in the United States

ABOUT THE AUTHOR

Dr. Tinjacá received her doctorate in psychology with a specialization in developmental and applied learning theory from the University of Kansas. Upon completion of her doctoral degree she accepted a position in organizational development with AlliedSignal, Inc., now Honeywell, in Kansas City, Missouri. After winning several performance awards and promotions within Allied, Mabel accepted a position as director of organization development at the Kauffman Center for Entrepreneurial Leadership at the Ewing Marion Kauffman Foundation in Kansas City, which gave her the opportunity to learn about entrepreneurs and high-growth companies.

When she decided to combine her interest in community development and knowledge about leadership and entrepreneurship with her desire to give back to the community, the idea for a book about Hispanic entrepreneurs was born.

Her company, Strategies for Growth, advises corporate, entrepreneurial and nonprofit organizations on improving their internal growth and development strategies. The Hispanic Entrepreneurs Project, or HEP, is a specialty within her practice that focuses on Hispanic business and nonprofit organizations.

Dr. Tinjacá has over 20 years' experience working with leaders in corporations, government agencies, entrepreneurial firms and non-profit organizations. She combines this experience with the leadership best practices and lessons learned from the entrepreneurs she interviewed to support the growth and development of business ventures.

For information about
presentations, corporate seminars,
board retreats and workshops;
to comments on ¡*Visión!* or
to order additional copies

contact:

Mabel Tinjacá, Ph.D.
Strategies for Growth
Hispanic Entrepreneurs Project (HEP)
(913) 327-11159
vision@kcnet.com

Be Involved in *¡Visión!*

B ecause there are so many Hispanic entrepreneurs and leaders that need to be recognized, we are planning on developing *¡Visión!* as a series of books. Every one to two years the statistics will be updated and one to three new entrepreneurs will be highlighted. We invite you to contribute to this process:

- Submit names of entrepreneurs and leaders you believe have a compelling story to tell. They can be individuals that have met significant challenges and have overcome them, or successful people whose wisdom and leadership deserves to be known.

- Tell us what you would like to know about the Hispanic community – its business, corporate, government or other leaders. What facts would be of interest to you?

- Share with us what you like about this book and we should continue in the series. Tell us what was not as useful, and you think we should change.

- Let us know if you, your organization or another organization would be interested in sponsoring one of the books in the series.

- Tell your friends, colleagues and family about this book and the planned series and ask them to contact us for any or all of the above.

Thank you for your interest in this project.

Muchas Gracias

Your Name _____

Address _____

Telephone number _____

E-mail address _____

❏ I nominate _____ to be highlighted
in the ¡*Visión!* series because:

_____
_____

This person can be reached at:

_____

❏ I am interested in reading more about:

_____

❏ Continue doing this:

_____

❏ Consider doing this:

_____

❏ I would be interested in sponsoring one of the books
in the series, call me or send me additional information.

❏ I think you should contact this organization for a
potential sponsorship:

_____

❏ I have told my friends and/or colleagues about
your series.

Gracias Nuevamente

Send this or e-mail information to:
¡Visión!
12909 W. 116th St. • Overland Park, KS 66210
mtinjaca@kcnet.com • (913) 338-3893 (fax)